JOHN MARSTON

THE SCOURGE OF VILLANIE
1599

ELIZABETHAN AND JACOBEAN QUARTOS

ELIZABETHAN AND JACOBEAN QUARTOS
EDITED BY G. B. HARRISON

JOHN MARSTON

THE SCOURGE OF VILLANIE

1599

BARNES & NOBLE, Inc.
New York, New York

This edition published in 1966
by Barnes & Noble, Inc.
is reproduced from the series
BODLEY HEAD QUARTOS
published by
John Lane The Bodley Head Ltd., London
between 1922 and 1926

Note

THE ORIGINAL of this
text is in the Bodleian Library
(8° L. 550. B.S.). The text
is reprinted line for line and
page for page, and similar
ornaments have been used.
A list of the misprints which
have been corrected will be
found on page 123.

G. B. H.

Printed in the United States of America

INTRODUCTION

THE SCOURGE OF VILLANIE is not a book to be read for pleasure or amusement. It is neither great literature nor even great satire. Its lines are usually turgid, allusions are most difficult to follow, and the whole, even for Elizabethan satire, is very liberally 'bescumbered.' But, for all that, neither the *Scourge* nor its author can be neglected by anyone who wishes to understand the mentality of English writers at the close of the sixteenth century.

Only the outline is known of Marston's life.[1] He was of gentle birth, his father being a member of the Inner Temple. On 4th February, 1592, he was admitted to Brasenose College, Oxford, where he took his B.A. two years later. Then he came to London to study law, which he soon found distasteful. In 1598, his *Metamorphosis of Pygmalion's Image: And certain Satires* was published, being followed in the autumn by the first edition of *The Scourge of Villanie*, of which a second edition was issued in 1599. A few months later, he began

---

[1] For the life of Marston, see the Introduction to A. H. Bullen's edition of *The Works of Marston*, 1887. A new edition of the complete works is badly needed. For short accounts of the Stage War, in which Marston was one of the principal combatants, see J. H. Penniman's edition of *Poetaster* and *Satiro-mastix*, and my *Shakespeare's Fellows*. See also *The Satire of John Marston*, by Morse S. Allen.

to write plays for the Children of Paul's, and in the next few years produced, amongst others, *Antonio and Mellida*, *Antonio's Revenge*, *What You Will* and *The Malcontent*. He married Mary, daughter of the Rev. William Wilks, Chaplain to King James the First, and the marriage seems to have been a success, as his wife, who survived him, desired in her will to be buried by his side. After 1607, he ceased to write for the stage, and little more is known of his movements for the next few years. Before 1616, however, he had taken Holy Orders, and from October, 1616, to September, 1631, he was Rector of Christ Church in Hampshire. He died in London on 25th June, 1634, and was buried beside his father in the Temple Church; his grave, so the story runs, being inscribed with two words—OBLIVIONI SACRVM.

Yet although Marston dedicated himself and his *Scourge* to Oblivion, it is quite clear, from the number of references to his work and, above all, from his prominence in the Stage War of 1599-1602, that he was deservedly conspicuous amongst popular writers of the day. Indeed, the man who wrote *The Malcontent* and *What You Will* was not far short of being a genius, however sombre.

It was rather the fashion amongst critics of the last generation to dismiss *The Scourge of Villanie* as exaggerated, insincere, and of no importance.

It may be so; but men who are capable of writing as Marston did at his best, are always worth studying, and it is not unreasonable, even in his early work, to take him at his word when he claims to be a genuine moralist and reformer. Young men of twenty-two frequently have a passion for reforming the world, though their methods differ according to their temperaments. Moreover, there is every indication that Marston was morbidly sincere, and perhaps in his own way even an idealist; for quite often your satirist is an idealist with his head in the mud.

Indeed, it is more than coincidence that Hall, Marston, and a third greater than either, John Donne, wrote satires in their youth and turned Churchmen in their maturity; for all three were men of keenly sensitive minds. Each passed through the same spiritual crisis, and each in the end looked for salvation on his knees.

But *The Scourge of Villanie* is not only important for its bearing on the personality of John Marston. It is a typical but extreme case of a mental disease, very prevalent at the time, and commonly known as the 'Melancholick Humour.' 'I have neither the scholar's melancholy, which is emulation,' says Jaques, 'nor the musician's, which is fantastical, nor the courtier's, which is proud, nor the soldier's, which is ambitious, nor the lawyer's, which is politic, nor the lady's, which is nice, nor the lover's, which is all these: but it is a melancholy of mine own, compounded of many simples, extracted from many objects, and indeed the sundry contemplation of my travels, in which my often rumination wraps me in a most humorous sadness.'

> '*Thou nursing Mother of faire wisedoms lore,*
> *Ingenuous Melancholy,* I implore
> Thy graue assistance,'
>
> > cries 'W. Kinsader.'

The student in future generations will be able to follow the play and clash of ideas in our England by simply reading the periodicals, because nearly every new idea finds its way into print and is there preserved. But in Marston's day there were no periodicals in which to vent the passing thought. Literary men lived the community life: they met their fellows often and intimately. New ideas were discussed in inns and taverns, and not in the correspondence columns of the *Spectator*. It follows that most of the passing moods of Elizabethan Englishmen have been irrecoverably lost. However, from what does remain, it is not difficult to trace the growth of an interest first in realism and then in psychology (in those days called 'anatomising') which begins in the early 1590's. It shows itself, for instance, in Sir John Davies, who published indecent society epigrams in 1593, and the highly introspective *Nosce teipsum* in 1599. The change is best epitomised in Greene's *Groatsworth of Witte* (1592), which starts as a romance and ends as a piece of stark, disillusioned realism. The appetite for romance grew jaded; *Mamillia* gave place to *The Disputation between a Hee Connycatcher and a Shee Connycatcher*. Greene was typical of his public, who were realizing with loathing and disgust that, however enticing and alluring Madam Lamilia might be in fiction, there was nothing but sordid reality to be found in the Bankside stews.

This change of interest is quite as noticeable on the stage: it appears in the drama of types of which the most familiar examples are the 'Humour Plays' of Ben Jonson.

From psychology and realism to satire the step is short. The Elizabethan observer, lacking the detachment of the modern scientist, found abnormal lust horrible and revolting, a thing to be hounded with vile epithets, and not a subject for dispassionate psycho-analysis.

The progress of this 'humour,' which began as a mild melancholy and ended as a diseased bitterness against the world in general and sex in particular, has often been traced in the plays of

Shakespeare. It passes from Jaques, who thanks his companions for making him melancholy, to the bitterness of Hamlet, to whom this goodly frame, the earth, appears no other thing than a pestilent congregation of vapours. It rises in the foul thoughts of Lear when his wits have turned until it reaches a climax of bitterness in Timon. Indeed, most of Shakespeare's biographers (with the conspicuous exception of Sir Sidney Lee) have been so puzzled by Shakespeare's 'tragic period' that they have sought explanation in some external crisis in Shakespeare's life. But Shakespeare's 'tragic period' is not unique: the same change of feeling and outlook occurs simultaneously in so many different places that its true explanation is to be found rather in the heart-sickness of the age than the personal sorrows of the individual. The plays of Ben Jonson are quite as bitter, and it appears strongly even in so popular and topical a play as *Eastward Ho*.

The main causes of this feeling of disillusionment are much the same as those which Dean Inge expresses in his essay on *The Victorian Age*. The great men who for so long had been associated with the glories of Elizabeth's reign were passing away and the new generation seemed to possess all their vices and none of their virtues. Hamlet sums it all up in his soliloquy on Death:

'For who would bear the whips and scorns of
    time,
The oppressor's wrong, the proud man's con-
    tumely,
The pangs of despized love, the law's delay,
The insolence of office, and the spurns
That patient merit of the unworthy takes,
When he himself might his quietus make
With a bare bodkin?'

These evils are very general: they exist in most
communities, but at this particular time they were
very vividly realized. Added to these, was a
revulsion of feeling against sensuality. In the full
tide of the Renaissance, Englishmen had un-
bridled their passions: with surfeit, they grew
ashamed.

Close parallels to Hamlet's melancholy and
Lear's madness will be found in *The Scourge of
Villanie*, though needless to say Marston does not
speak in Shakespeare's 'fine filed phrase'; he
snarls far more bitterly on his own peculiar dunghill. But the same sentiments are there, as a short
summary will show.

The first three satires are chiefly concerned with
various aspects of immorality and unnatural vice,
including an attack on those who use religion as
a cloak for self-advancement. The fourth gives a
few pictures of those who propose to repent—

to-morrow. The fifth shows the advantages of 'sleight' as the only means of promotion. In the sixth, which is comparatively amusing, Marston hits out at various types of contemporary poet. In the seventh, he denounces the gallant who is nothing but clothes, and the abuses of the law's delays; in the eighth the extravagance of love-sick poets. This leads on to an attack on various literary rivals in the ninth satire. Finally, in the tenth, which is also the best, he caricatures some familiar types of Elizabethan gallant.

The Scourge of Villanie was a popular book which reflected the taste and probably the affected jargon[1] of the fashionable circles in which Marston moved. As usually happens, when a society satire is published, there were many attempts to identify the originals. Some indeed seem still to be recognizable; but for the most part it is unprofitable labour trying to fit real names to the not uncommon types which Marston satirised. Many of them are still with us. There are plenty of Luxurios in every age; Martius no longer worries his Livia by demonstrating 'the ward by *puncta reuersa*,' he now teaches her how to putt; Torquatus has exchanged his Angelica for a motor-bike; while 'iudiciall' Musus, who now reviews books for the periodicals, seems not

---

[1] *See* Marston's own remarks on p. 10.

to have changed at all.[1] Besides, Marston himself has expressly warned us in his epilogue 'To him that hath perused me' not to cast our eyes upon privateness—a paragraph curiously reminiscent of what Jaques said on a similar occasion.[2]

The first edition of *The Scourge of Villanie*, containing nine satires, was entered in the Stationers' Register on 8th September, 1598. A second, 'corrected' edition, from which our text has been reprinted, was issued with the addition of the tenth satire in 1599. Its further progress was, however, summarily stopped by the drastic measures taken in June, 1599, to stop scurrilous pamphleteering when the Archbishop of Canterbury issued orders that all books of a satirical or indecent nature should be seized and burnt. Both *Pygmalion* and *The Scourge* formed part of the bonfire in the yard of Stationers' Hall.

King's College,   G. B. HARRISON
    University of London.

---

[1] pp. 108–111.
[2] *See* Note on p. 124.

THE
SCOVRGE OF
Villanie.

Corrected, with the addition of
newe Satyres.

Three Bookes of Satyres.
(***)

PERSIVS.
v v v Nec scombros metuentia carmina, nec thus.

AT LONDON,
Printed by I. R. Anno Dom.
1599. *Edit 1598.*

To his moſt eſteemed, and beſt
beloued Selfe,

DAT DEDICATQVE.

To *Detraction* I present my *Poesie*.

FOule canker of faire vertuous action,
Vile blaster of the freshest bloomes on earth,
Enuies abhorred child *Detraction*,
I heare expose, to thy all-taynting breath
The issue of my braine, snarle, raile, barke, bite,
Know that my spirit scornes *Detractions* spight.

Know that the *Genius*, which attendeth on,
And guides my powers intellectuall,
Holds in all vile repute *Detraction*,
My soule an essence metaphisicall,
That in the basest sort scornes *Critickes* rage,
Because he knowes his sacred parentage.

My

To Detraction.

My spirit is not puft vp with fatte fume
Of slimie Ale, nor *Bacchus* heating grape.
My minde disdaines the dungie muddy scum
Of abiect thoughts, and *Enuies* raging hate.
  True iudgement, slight regards Opinion,
  A sprightly wit, disdaines Detraction.

A partiall prayse shall neuer eleuate
My setled censure, of mine owne esteeme.
A cankered verdit of malignant Hate
Shall nere prouoke me, worse my selfe to deeme.
  Spight of despight, and rancors villanie,
  I am my selfe, so is my poesie.

In Lectores prorsus indignos.

FY Satyre fie, shall each mechanick slaue,
   Each dunghill pesant, free perusall haue
   Of thy well labor'd lines? Each sattin sute,
   Each quaint fashion-monger, vvhose sole re-
Rests in his trim gay clothes, lie slauering (pute
Taynting thy lines with his lewd censuring?
Shall each odde puisne of the Lawyers Inne,
Each barmy-froth, that last day did beginne
To reade his little, or his *nere a whit*,
Or shall some greater auntient, of lesse wit,
(That neuer turn'd but browne Tobacco leaues
Whose sences some damn'd *Occupant* bereaues)
Lye gnawing on thy vacant times expence?
Tearing thy rimes, quite altering the sence?
Or shall perfum'd *Castilio* censure thee?
Shall he oreview thy sharpe-fang'd poesie?
(Who nere read further then his Mistris lips)
Nere practiz'd ought, but som spruce capring skips
                               Nere

In Lectores prorsus indignos.

Nere in his life did other language vse,
But *Sweet Lady, faire Mistres, kind hart, deere couse,*
Shall this *Fantasma*, this *Colosse* peruse
And blast with stinking breath, my budding Muse?
Fie, wilt thou make thy wit a Curtezan
For euery broking hand-crafts artizan?
Shall brainlesse Cyterne heads, each iobernole,
Poket the very *Genius* of thy soule?
  I *Phylo*, I, I'le keepe an open hall,
A common, and a sumptuous festiuall,
Welcome all eyes, all eares, all tongues to me,
Gnaw pesants on my scraps of Poesie.
Castilios, Cyprians, court-boyes, spanish blocks,
Ribanded eares, granado-netherstocks,
Fidlers, Scriueners, pedlers, tynkering knaues,
Base blew-coats, tapsters, broad-cloth minded slaues
Welcome I-fayth, but may you nere depart,
Till I haue made your gauled hides to smart.
                                    Your

4

Your gauled hides? avaunt base muddy scum.
Thinke you a Satyres dreadfull sounding drum
Will brace it selfe? and daine to terrefie,
Such abiect pesants basest rogary?
No, no, passe on ye vaine fantasticke troupe
Of puffie youthes; Know I doe scorne to stoupe
To rip your liues. Then hence lewd nags, away,
Goe read each post, view what is plaid to day.
Then to *Priapus* gardens. You *Castilio*,
I pray thee let my lines in freedome goe,
Let me alone, the Madams call for thee,
Longing to laugh at thy wits pouerty.
Sirra, liuorie cloake, you lazie slipper slaue,
Thou fawning drudge, what would'st thou Satyres
Base mind away, thy master calls, begon, (haue?
Sweet *Gnato* let my poesie alone.
Goe buy some ballad of the Faiery King,
And of the begger vvench, some rogie thing,

    B 1.   Which

In Lectores prorsus indignos.

Which thou maist chaunt vnto the chamber-maid
To some vile tune, when that thy Maister's laid.
   But will you needs stay? am I forc'd to beare,
The blasting breath of each lewd Censurer?
Must naught but clothes, and images of men
But sprightles truncks, be Iudges of thy pen?
Nay then come all, I prostitute my Muse,
For all the swarme of Idiots to abuse.
Reade all, view all, euen with my full consent,
So you will know that which I neuer meant;
So you will nere conceiue, and yet dispraise,
That which you nere conceiu'd, & laughter raise:
Where I but striue in honest seriousnes,
To scourge some soule-poluting beastlines.
So you will raile, and finde huge errors lurke
In euery corner of my Cynick worke.
Proface, reade on, for your extreamst dislikes
Will add a pineon, to my praises flights.

O,

In Lectores prorsus indignos.

O, how I bristle vp my plumes of pride,
O, how I thinke my Satyres dignifi'd,
When I once heare some quaint *Castilio*,
Some supple mouth'd slaue, some lewd *Tubrio*,
Some spruce pedant, or some span-new come fry
Of Innes a-court, striuing to vilefie
My dark reproofes. Then doe but raile at me,
No greater honor craues my poesie.

  1. But yee diuiner wits, celestiall soules,
        Whose free-borne mindes no kennel thought
  Ye sacred spirits, *Mayas* eldest sonnes. (controules,

  2. Yee substance of the shadowes of our age,
        In whom all graces linke in marriage,
  To you how cheerfully my Poem runnes.

In Lectores prorsus indignos.

3. True iudging eyes, quick sighted censurers,
    Heauens best beauties, wisedoms treasurers,
O how my loue embraceth your great worth.

4. Yee Idols of my soule, ye blessed spirits,
    How shold I giue true honor to your merrits
Which I can better thinke, then here paint forth.

You sacred spirits, *Maias* eldest sonnes,
To you how cheerefully my poeme runnes.
O how my loue, embraceth your great worth,
Which I can better think, then here paint forth.

O rare!

¶ To

✱ To those that seeme iudiciall perusers.

KNow I hate to affect too much obscurity, & harshnes, because they profit no sence. To note vices, so that no man can vnderstand them, is as fond, as the French execution in picture. Yet there are some, (too many) that think nothing good, that is so curteous, as to come within their reach. Tearming all Satyres (bastard) which are not palpable darke, and so rough writ, that the hearing of them reade, would set a mans teeth on edge. For whose vnseasond pallate I wrote the first Satyre in some places too obscure, in all places mislyking me. Yet whẽ by some scuruy chance it shall come into the late perfumed fist of iudiciall *Torquatus*, (that like some rotten stick in a troubled water, hath gotte a great deale of barmy froth to stick to his sides) I know he will vouchsafe it, some of his new-minted Epithets, (as *Reall, Intrinsecate, Delphicke,*) when in my conscience he vnderstands not the least part of it. But from thence proceedes his iudgement. *Persius* is crabby, because antient, & his ierks, (being perticulerly giuen to

To the iudiciall peruser.

priuate customes of his time) dusky. *Iuvenall* (vpon the like occasion) seemes to our iudgement, gloomy. Yet both of them goe a good seemely pace, not stumbling, shufling. *Chaucer* is hard even to our vnderstandings: who knowes not the reason? how much more those old Satyres which expresse themselues in terms, that breathed not long euen in theyr dayes. But had we then liued, the vnderstanding of them had beene nothing hard. I will not deny there is a seemely decorum to be obserued, and a peculier kinde of speech for a Satyres lips, which I can willinglier conceaue, then dare to prescribe; yet let me haue the substance rough, not the shadow. I cannot, nay I will not delude your sight with mists; yet I dare defend my plainnes gainst the veriuyce face, of the crabbed'st Satyrist that euer stuttered. Hee that thinks worse of my rimes then my selfe, I scorne him, for he cannot, he that thinks better, is a foole. So fauour mee *Good-Opinion*, as I am farre from being a *Suffenus*. If thou perusest me with an vnpartiall eye, reade on, if otherwise, know I neither value thee, nor thy censure. *VV. Kinsayder.*

PROEMIVM IN

librum primum.

I Beare the scourge of iust *Rhamnusia*,
Lashing the lewdnes of *Britania*.
Let others sing as their good *Genius* moues,
Of deepe designes, or else of clipping loues.
Faire fall them all, that with wits industry,
Doe cloath good subiects in true poesie.
But as for me, my vexed thoughtfull soule,
Takes pleasure, in displeasing sharp controule.
   Thou nursing Mother of faire wisedoms lore,
Ingenuous Melancholly, I implore
Thy graue assistance, take thy gloomy seate,
Inthrone thee in my blood; Let me intreate

Stay

Proemium in librum primum.

Stay his quicke iocond skips, and force him runne
A sadde pac'd course, vntill my whips be done.
Daphne, vnclip thine armes from my sad brow,
Blacke Cypresse crowne me whilst I vp doe plow
The hidden entrailes of ranke villanie.
Tearing the vaile from damn'd impietie.
    Quake guzzell dogs, that liue on putred slime,
    Skud from the lashes of my yerking rime.

S A-

SATYRE. I.
Fronti nulla fides.

MArry God forfend, *Martius* swears he'le stab,
Phrigeo, feare not, thou art no lying drab.
What though dagger hack'd mouthes of his blade
It slew as many as figures of yeeres   (sweares
Aqua fortis eate in't, or as many more,
As methodist *Musus*, kild with Hellebore
In autumne last, yet he beares the male lye
With as smooth calme, as *Mecho* riualrie.
How ill his shape, with inward forme doth fage,
Like *Aphrogenias* ill-yok'd marriage.
Fond Physiognomer, *Complexion*
Guides not the inward disposition,
Inclines I yeeld. Thou sayst Law *Iulia*,⎫
Or *Catoes* often curst *Scatinia*   ⎬
Can take no hold on simpring *Lesbia*, ⎭
True, not on her eye, yet Allom oft doth blast,
The sprouting bud that faine would longer last.
Cary

Fronti nulla fides.

Chary *Casca*, right pure or *Rhodanus*,
Yet each night drinks in glassie Priapus.
   Yon Pine is faire, yet fouly doth it ill
To his owne sprouts, marke, his rank drops distill
Foule Naples canker in their tender rinde!
Woe worth when trees drop in their proper kinde!
Mystagogus, what meanes this prodigy?
When *Hiadolgo* speakes gainst vsury.
When *Verres* railes gainst thieues. *Mylo* doth hate
Murder, *Clodius* cuckolds, *Marius* the gate
Of squinting *Ianus* shuts? runne beyond bound
Of *Nil vltra*, and hang me when on's found
Will be himselfe. Had Nature turn'd our eyes
Into our proper selues, these curious spies
Would be asham'd, *Flauia* would blush to flout
When *Oppia* calls *Lucina* helpe her out.
If she did thinke, *Lynceus* did know her ill,
How Nature, Art, how Art, doth Nature spill.
God

Fronti nulla fides.

God pardon me, I often did auer
Quod gratis, *grate*, the Astronomer
An honest man, but I'le doe so no more,
His face deceau'd me; but now since his whore
And sister are all one, his honestie
Shall be as bare as his Anatomie,
To which he bound his vvife, ô packstaffe rimes!
vvhy not, when court of starrs shall see these crimes?
Rodds are in pisse, I for thee *Empericke*,
That twenty graines of *Oppium* wilt not sticke
To minister to babes. Heer's bloody dayes,
When with plaine hearbes, *Mutius* more men slaies
Then ere third *Edwards* sword. Sooth in our age,
Mad *Coribantes* neede not to enrage
The peoples mindes. You *Ophiogine*
Of *Hellespont*, with vvrangling villanie
The swolne world's inly stung, then daine a touch,
If that your fingers can effect so much.

                                                  Thou

Fronti nulla fides.

Thou sweet Arabian *Panchaia*,
Perfume this nastie age, smugge *Lesbia*
Hath stinking lunges, although a simpring grace,
A muddy inside, though a surphul'd face.
O for some deepe-searching *Corycean*,
To ferret out yon lewd *Cynedian*.
　How now *Brutus*, what shape best pleaseth thee?
All *Protean* formes, thy wife in venery
At thy inforcement takes; vvell goe thy way,
Shee may transforme thee ere thy dying day.
Hush, *Gracchus* heares, that hath retaild more lyes,
Broched more slaunders, done more villanies,
Then *Fabius* perpetuall golden coate
(Which might haue *Semper idem* for a mott)
Hath beene at feasts, and led the measuring
At Court, and in each marriage reueling,
Writ *Palæphatus*, comment on those dreames,
That *Hylus* takes, mid'st dung-pit reeking steames
　　　　　　　　　　　　　　　　　Of

16

Fronti nulla fides.

Of *Athos* hote house. Gramercie modest smyle.
Chremes a sleepe. *Paphia*, sport the while.
Lucia, new set thy ruffe, tut thou art pure,
Canst thou not lispe, (*good brother*) looke demure?
Fye *Gallus*, vvhat, a Skeptick *Pyrrhomist*?
When chast *Dictinna*, breakes the Zonelike twist?
Tut, hang vp *Hieroglyphickes*. Ile not faine
Wresting my humor, from his natiue straine.

SATYRE. II.
Difficile est Satyram non scribere.

v v v-- Iuve.

J Cannot hold, I cannot I indure
　　To view a big womb'd foggie clowde immure
The radiant tresses of the quickning sunne.
Let Custards quake, my rage must freely runne.
Preach

Difficile est Satyram non scribere.

Preach not the Stoickes patience to me,
I hate no man, but mens impietie.
My soule is vext, what power will'th desist?
Or dares to stop a sharpe fangd Satyrist?
Who'le coole my rage? whole stay my itching fist,
But I will plague and torture whom I list?
If that the three-fold walls of Babilon
Should hedge my tongue, yet I should raile vpon
This fustie world, that now dare put in vre
To make *IEHOVA* but a couerture,
To shade ranck filth, *loose conscience is free,*
From all conscience, what els hath libertie?
As't please the Thracian Boreas to blow,
So turnes our ayerie conscience, to, and fro.

What icye *Saturnist,* what Northerne pate
But such grosse lewdnes would exasperate?
I thinke the blind doth see, the flame God rise
From sisters couch, each morning to the skies:

Glow-

Difficile est Satyram non scribere.

Glowing vvith lust. VValke but in duskie night,
With *Linceus* eyes, and to thy piercing sight
Disguised Gods vvill show, in pesants shape,
Prest to commit some execrable rape.
Here *Ioues* lust pander, *Maias* iugling sonne,
In clownes disguise, doth after milk-maides runne.
And fore he'le loose his brutish lechery,
The truls shall tast sweet Nectars surquedry.
There *Iunos* brat, forsakes *Neries* bed,
And like a swaggerer, lust fiered,
Attended onely with his smock sworne page,
Pert *Gallus*, slilie slippes along, to wage
Tilting incounters, with some spurious seede
Of marrow pyes, and yawning Oystars breede.
O damn'd!

Who would not shake a Satyres knottie rod?
When to defile the sacred seate of God

Is

Difficile est Satyram non scribere.

Is but accounted Gentlemens disport?
To snort in filth, each hower to resort
To brothell pits; alas a veniall crime,
Nay, royall, to be last in *thirtith* slime.
   Ay me, hard world for Satyrists beginne
To sette vp shop, when no small petty sinne
Is left vnpurg'd, once to bee pursie fat
Had wont be cause that life did macerate.
Marry the iealous Queene of ayre doth frowne,
That Ganimede is vp, and Hebe downe.
Once *Albion* liu'd in such a cruell age
That men did hold by seruile villenage. (borne,
Poore brats vvere slaues, of bond-men that vvere
And marted, sold, but that rude law is torne,
And disanuld, as too too inhumane,
That Lords ore pesants should such seruice straine.
But now, (sad change) the kennell sincke of slaues,
Pesant great Lords, and seruile seruice craues.

                                 Bond-

Difficile est Satyram non scribere.

Bondslaues sonnes had wont be bought & sold,
But now *Heroes* heires (if they haue not told
A discreet number, fore theyr dad did die)
Are made much of, how much from merchandie?
Tail'd, and retail'd, till to the pedlers packe,
The fourth-hand ward-ware comes, alack, alack,
Would truth did know I lyed, but truth, and I,
Doe know that sence is borne to misery.
Oh wold to God, this were their worst mischance,
vvere not theyr soules sold to darke ignorance.
Faire goodnes is foule ill, if mischiefes wit
Be not represt from lewd corrupting it.

   O what dry braine melts not sharp mustard rime
To purge the snottery of our slimie time?
Hence idle *Cave*, vengeance pricks me on,
When mart is made of fayre Religion,
Reform'd bald *Trebus* swore, in Romish quiere
He sold Gods essence for a poore denier.
              C.   The

Difficile est Satyram non scribere.

The Egyptians adored Onions,
To Garlike yeelding all deuotions.
O happy Garlick, but thrice happy you,
Whose senting gods, in your large gardens grew.
Democritus, rise from thy putrid slime
Sport at the madnes of that hotter clime.
Deride their frenzy, that for pollicie
Adore Wheate dough, as reall deitie.
Almighty men, that can their Maker make,
And force his sacred body to forsake
The Cherubines, to be gnawne actually,
Deuiding *indiuiduum*, really.
Making a score of Gods with one poore word,
I, so I thought, in that you could afford,
So cheape a penny-worth. O ample fielde,
In which a Satyre may iust weapon weelde.
But I am vext, when swarmes of *Iulians*
Are still manur'd by lewd Precisians.

Who

Difficile est Satyram non scribere.

Who scorning Church rites, take the simbole vp
As slouenly, as carelesse Courtiers slup
Their mutton gruell. Fie, who can with-hold,
But must of force make his mild Muse a scold?
When that he greeued sees, with red vext eyes,
That Athence antient large immunities,
Are eye sores to the fates; Poore cells forlorne!
Ist not enough you are made an abiect scorne
To iering Apes, but must the shadow too
Of auncient substance, be thus wrung from you?
O split my hart, least it doe breake with rage
To see th'immodest loosenes of our age.
Immodest loosenes? fie too gentle word,
When euery signe can brothelry afford.
When lust doth sparkle from our females eyes
And modesty is rousted in the skyes.
    Tell me *Galliottæ*, what meanes this signe
When impropriat gentiles will turne *Capuchine?*
                    C 2   Sooner

Difficile est Satyram non scribere.

Sooner be damn'd. O stuffe Satyricall?
vvhen rapine feedes our pomp, pomp ripes our fall.
When the guest trembles at his hosts swart looke,
The sonne, doth feare his stepdame, that hath tooke
His mothers place for lust, the twin-borne brother
Malinges his mate, that first came from his mother.
When to be huge, is to be deadly sicke,
When vertuous pesants, will not spare to lick
The deuils tayle for poore promotion.
When for neglect, slubbred *Deuotion*
Is wan with greefe. When *Rufus*, yawnes for death
Of him that gaue him vndeserued breath.
When *Hermus* makes a worthy question,
Whether of *Wright*, as *Paraphonalion*
A siluer pispot fits his Lady dame?
Or i'st too good? a pewter best became.
When *Agrippina* poysons *Claudius* sonne,
That all the world to her own brat might run.
vvhen

Difficile est Satyram non scribere.

whẽ the husband, gapes that his stale wife wold die,
That he might once be in by *curtesie*.   (death
The big paunch'd wife, longs for her loth'd mates
That she might haue more ioyntures here on earth.
When tenure for short yeeres, (by many a one)
Is thought right good be turn'd forth *Littleton*,
All to be *headdie*, or *free-hold* at least,
When tis all one, for long life be a beast,
A slaue, as haue a short term'd tenancie
vvhen dead's the strength of Englands yeomanrie,
When invndation of luxuriousnes,
Fatts all the vvorld vvith such grosse beastlines.
Who can abstaine? what modest braine can hold,
But he must make his shamefac'd Muse a scold?

SATYRE. III.

Redde, age, quæ deinceps risisti.

IT's good be warie whilst the sunne shines cleere
(Quoth that old chuffe that may dispend by yere
Three thousand pound) whilst hee of good pre-
Cõmits himselfe to Fleet to saue expence. (tence
No Countries Christmas: rather tarry heere,
The Fleet is cheap, the Country hall too deere.
But *Codrus*, harke, the world expects to see
Thy bastard heire rotte there in misery.
What? vvill *Luxurio* keepe so great a hall
That he will proue a bastard in his fall?
No, *come on fiue, S. George, by heauen at all*,
Makes his catastrophe, right tragicall;
At all, till nothing's left, *Come on*, till all comes off,
I haire and all, *Luxurio*, left a scoffe
To leaprous filths: ô stay, thou impious slaue,
Teare not the lead from off thy Fathers graue,

To

Redde, age, quæ deinceps risisti.

To stop base brokage, sell not thy fathers sheete,
His leaden sheete, that strangers eyes may greete
Both putrefaction of thy greedy Sire,
And thy abhorred viperous desire.
But wilt thou needs, shall thy Dads lacky brat
Weare thy Sires halfe-rot finger in his hat?
Nay then *Luxurio* waste in obloquy,
And I shall sport to heare thee faintly cry,
A die, a drab, and filthy broking knaues,
Are the worlds wide mouthes, all deuouring graues.
Yet *Samus* keepes a right good house I heare;
No, it keepes him, and free'th him from chill feare
Of shaking fitts; How then shall his smug wench,
How shall her bawd, (fit time) assist her quench
Her sanguine heate? *Linceus*, canst thou sent?
Shee hath her Monkey, & her instrument
Smooth fram'd at *Vitrio*. O greeuous misery!
Luscus hath left her female luxury.

I

Redde, age, quæ deinceps risisti.

I, it left him; No, his old Cynick Dad
Hath forc'd him cleane forsake his Pickhatch drab.
Alack, alack, vvhat peece of lustfull flesh
Hath *Luscus* left, his *Priape* to redresse?
Grieue not good soule, he hath his *Ganimede*,
His perfum'd she-goat, smooth kembd & high fed.
At Hogsdon now his monstrous lust he feasts,
For there he keepes a baudy-house of beasts.
Paphus, let *Luscus* haue his Curtezan,
Or we shall haue a monster of a man.
Tut, *Paphus* now detaines him from that bower,
And claspes him close within his brick-built tower.
Diogenes, th'art damn'd for thy lewd wit,
For *Luscus* now hath skill to practise it.
Fayth, what cares he for faire *Cynedian* boyes?
Veluet cap'd Goates, duch Mares? tut cõmon toies.
Detaine them all, on this condition
He may but vse the Cynick friction.

O

28

Redde, age, quæ deinceps risisti.

O now yee male stewes, I can giue pretence
For your luxurious incontinence.
Hence, hence, yee falsed, seeming, Patriotes,
Returne not vvith pretence of saluing spots,
When here yee soyle vs with impuritie,
And monstrous filth of Doway seminary.
What though *Iberia* yeeld you liberty,
To snort in source of Sodome vilanie?
VVhat though the bloomes of young nobilitie,
Committed to your *Rodons* custodie,
Yee *Nero* like abuse? yet nere approch,
Your new S. *Homers* lewdnes heere to broch;
Taynting our Townes, and hopefull Accademes,
With your lust-bating most abhorred meanes.
  Valladolid, our Athence gins to tast
Of thy ranck filth, Camphire and Lettuce chast,
Are cleane casheird, now *Sophi* Ringoes eate,
Candid Potatoes, are Athenians meate.

Hence

Redde, age, quæ deinceps risisti.

Hence Holy-thistle, come sweet marrow pie,
Inflame our backs to itching luxurie.
A Crabs bak'd guts, a Lobsters butterd thigh,
I heare them sweare is blood for venerie.
Had I some snout faire brats, they should indure
The new found *Castilian* callenture,
Before some pedant Tutor in his bed
Should vse my frie, like Phrigian *Ganimede*.
Nay then chast cells, when greasie *Aretine*,
For his ranck *Fico*, is sirnam'd diuine:
Nay then come all yee veniall scapes to me,
I dare well warrant you'le absolued be.
Rufus, I'le terme thee but intemperate,
I will not once thy vice exaggerate,
Though that each howre thou lewdly swaggerest,
And all the quarter day, pay'st interest
For the forbearance of thy chalked score.
Though that thou keep'st a tally with thy whore.
Since

Redde, age, quæ deinceps risisti.

Since *Nero* keepes his mother *Agrippine*,
And no strange lust can satiate *Messaline*,
 Tullus goe scotfree, though thou often bragg'st
That for a *false French-crowne*, thou vaulting hadst,
Though that thou know'st for thy incontinence
Thy drab repayd thee, *true French pestilence.*
But tush, his boast I beare, vvhen *Tegeran*
Brags that hee foysts his rotten Curtezan
Vpon his heire, that must haue all his lands:
And them hath ioyn'd in *Hymens* sacred bands.
Ile wincke at *Robrus*, that for vicenage
Enters commen, on his next neighbors stage,
When *Ioue* maintaines his sister and his whore;
And she incestuous, iealous euermore,
Least that *Europa* on the Bull should ride:
Woe worth when beasts for filth are deified!
 Alacke poore rogues, what Censor interdicts
The veniall scapes of him that purses picks?
            When

Redde, age, quæ deinceps risisti.

VVhen some slie golden-slopt *Castilio*
Can cut a manors strings at Primero?
Or with a pawne, shall giue a Lordship mate.
In statute staple chaining fast his state?
  What Academicke starued Satyrist
Would gnaw rez'd Bacon, or with inke black fist
would tosse each muck-heap for som outcast scraps
Of halfe-dung bones to stop his yawning chaps?
Or with a hungry hollow halfe pin'd iaw   (gnaw
VVould once a thrice-turn'd bone-pick'd subiect
When swarmes of Mountebancks, & Bandeti
Damn'd Briareans, sincks of villanie,
Factors for lewdnes, brokers for the deuill,
Infect our soules with all polluting euill.
  Shal *Lucea* scorne her husbands luke-warme bed?
(Because her pleasure being hurried
In ioulting Coach, with glassie instrument,
Doth farre exceede the *Paphian* blandishment)
                                        Whilst

32

Redde, age, quæ deinceps risisti.

Whilst I (like to some mute *Pythagoran*)
Halter my hate, and cease to curse and ban
Such brutish filth? Shall *Matho* raise his name,
By printing pamphlets in anothers name,
And in them praise himselfe, his wit, his might.
All to be deem'd his Countries Lanthorne light?
Whilst my tongue's ty'de with bonds of blushing
For feare of broching my concealed name? (shame
Shall *Balbus*, the demure Athenian,
Dreame of the death of next *Vicarian?*
Cast his natiuity? marke his complexion?
Waigh well his bodies weake condition?
That with guilt sleight he may be sure to get
The Planets place, when his dim shine shall set?
  Shall *Curio* streake his lims on his dayes couch,
In Sommer bower? and with bare groping touch
Incense his lust, consuming all the yeere
In *Cyprian* dalliance, and in *Belgick* cheere?
                                        Shall

Redde, age, quæ deinceps risisti.

Shall *Faunus* spend a hundred gallions,
Of Goates pure milke, to laue his stallions,
As much Rose iuyce? O bath! ô royall, ritch
To scower *Faunus*, and his salt proude bitch;
And when all's cleansd, shal the slaues inside stinck
worse thẽ the new cast slime of *Thames* ebd brink?
Whilst I securely let him ouer-slip?
Nere yerking him with my Satyricke whyp?

    Shall *Crispus* vvith hipocrisie beguile,
Holding a candle to some fiend a while?
Now Iew, then Turke, then seeming Christian,
Then Athiest, Papist, and straight Puritan,
Now nothing, any thing, euen what you list,
So that some guilt may grease his greedy fist?

    Shall *Damas* vse his third-hand ward as ill
As any iade that tuggeth in the mill?
What, shall law, nature, vertue, be reiected,
Shall these world Arteries be foule infected,

                      With

Redde, age, quæ deinceps risisti.

With corrupt blood? Whilst I shal *Martia* taske?
Or some young *Villius*, all in choller aske,
How he can keepe a lazie wayting man,
And buy a hoode, and siluer-handled fan
With fortie pound? Or snarle at *Lollios* sonne?
That with industrious paines hath harder wonne
His true got worship, and his gentries name
Then any Swine-heards brat, that lousie came
To luskish Athence, and with farming pots,
Compiling beds, and scouring greasie spots,
By chaunce (when he can like taught Parrat cry
Deerely belou'd, vvith simpering grauitie)
Hath got the Farme of some gelt Vicary,
And now on cock-horse, gallops iollilie;
Tickling with some stolne stuffe his sencelesse cure,
Belching lewd termes gainst all sound littrature.
Shall I with shaddowes fight? taske bitterly
Romes filth? scraping base channell rogarie?
                                        Whilst

Redde, age, quæ deinceps risisti.

Whilst such huge Gyants shall affright our eyes
With execrable, damn'd impieties?
Shall I finde trading *Mecho*, neuer loath
Frankly to take a damning periur'd oath?
Shall *Furia* broke her sisters modesty,
And prostitute her soule to brothelry?
Shall *Cossus* make his well-fac'd wife a stale,
To yeeld his braided ware a quicker sale?   stocks
Shall cock-horse, fat-paunch'd *Milo* staine whole
Of well borne soules, with his adultering spots?
Shall broking pandars sucke Nobility?
Soyling faire stems with foule impurity?
Nay, shall a trencher slaue extenuate,
Some *Lucrece* rape? and straight magnificate
Lewd *Iouian* lust? Whilst my satyrick vaine
Shall muzled be, not daring out to straine
His tearing paw? No gloomy *Iuvenall*,
Though to thy fortunes I disastrous fall.

                                        S A-

SATYRE. IIII.

CRAS.

I Marry Sir, here's perfect honesty:
When *Martius* will forsweare all villany:
(All damn'd abuse, of payment in the warres
  All filching from his Prince, and Souldiers)
When once he can but so much bright durt gleane,
As may mainetaine, one more White-friers queane.
One drab more, faith then farewell villany,
He'le cleanse himselfe to Shoredith purity.

  As for *Stadius*, I thinke he hath a soule,
And if he were but free from sharpe controule
Of his sower host, and from his Taylors bill,
He would not thus abuse his riming skill,
Iading our tyred eares with fooleries,
Greasing great slaues, with oylie flatteries,
Good faith I think, he would not striue to sute
The back of humorous Time, (for base repute
D.   Mong

CRAS.

Mong dunghill pesants) botching vp such ware,
As may be salable in Sturbridge fare.
If he were once but freed from specialty,
But sooth, till then, beare with his balladry.

I ask'd lewd *Gallus* when he'le cease to sweare,
And with whole culuering raging othes to teare
The vault of heauen, spetting in the eyes
Of natures Nature, lothsome blasphemies.
To morrow he doth vow he will forbeare:
Next day I meete him, but I heare him sweare
Worse then before, I put his vow in minde,
He aunswers me, *to morrow*, but I finde
He sweares next day, farre worse then ere before:
Putting me of with (*morrow*) euermore.
Thus when I vrge him, with his sophistrie
He thinks to salue his damned periurie.

Sylenus now is old, I wonder I
He doth not hate his triple venerie,

Cold,

CRAS.

Cold, writhled Eld, his liues-wet almost spent,
Me thinks a vnity were competent:
But ô faire hopes! He whispers secretly,
When it leaues him, he'le leaue his lechery.
　When simpring *Flaccus* (that demurely goes
Right neatly tripping on his new blackt toes)
Hath made rich vse of his Religion,
Of God himselfe, in pure deuotion:
When that the strange *Ideas* in his head
(Broched mongst curious sots, by shaddowes led)
Hath furnish'd him, by his hote auditors
Of faire demeanes, and goodly rich mannors,
Sooth then he will repent, when's treasury
Shall force him to disclaime his heresie.
What will not poore neede force? but being sped,
God for vs all, the gurmonds paunch is fed.
His mind is chang'd, but when will he doe good?
To morrow, (*I, to morrow by the rood.*)
D 2

Yet

CRAS.

Yet *Ruscus* sweares, he'le cease to broke a sute:
By peasant meanes striuing to get repute
Mong puffie Spunges, when the Fleet's defrayd
His reuell tier, and his Laundresse payd.
There is a crew which I too plaine could name
If so I might without th' *Aquinians* blame,
That lick the tayle of greatnes with their lips:
Laboring with third-hand iests, and Apish skips,
Retayling others wit, long barrelled
To glib some great mans eares, till panch be fed,
Glad if themselues, as sporting fooles be made,
To get the shelter of some high-growne shade.
To morrow yet these base tricks thei'le cast off,
And cease for lucar be a iering scoffe.
Ruscus will leaue, whence once he can renue
His wasted clothes, that are asham'd to view
The worlds proud eyes. *Drusus* will cease to fawne
vvhen that his Farme, that leakes in melting pawne
Some

CRAS.

Some Lord-applauded iest hath once set free.
All will *to morrow* leaue their roguerie.
When fox-furd *Mecho* (by damn'd vsury,
Cutthrote deceit, and his crafts villany)
Hath rak'd together some foure thousand pound,
To make his smug gurle, beare a bumming sound
In a young merchants eare, faith then (may be)
He'le ponder if there be Deitie?
Thinking if to the parrish pouerty,
At his wisht death, be dol'd a halfe-penny,
A worke of Supererogation,
A good filth-cleansing strong purgation.
  Aulus will leaue begging Monopolies,
When that mong troopes of gaudy Butter-flies,
He is but able iet it iollily,
In pie-bauld sutes of proud Court brauery.
  To morrow doth *Luxurio* promise me,
He will vnline himselfe from bitcherie.

                                   Marry

CRAS.

Marry *Alcides* thirteenth act must lend
A glorious period, and his lust-itch end.
When once he hath froth-foming Ætna past
At one and thirty being alwayes last.
    If not to *Day* (quoth that *Nasonian*)
Much lesse *to morrowe*, Yes saith *Fabian*,
For ingrain'd Habites, *died with often dips*,
Are not so soone discoloured, young slips
New set, are easily mou'd, and pluck'd away,
But elder rootes, clip faster in the clay.
I smile at thee, and at the Stagerite,
Who holds the liking of the appetite,
Being fed with actions often put in vre
Hatcheth the soule, in quality impure,
Or pure. May be in vertue, but for vice,
That comes by inspiration, with a trice
Young *Furius* scarce fifteene yeres of age
But is straight-wayes, right fit for mariage

                       Vnto

CRAS.

Vnto the deuill, for sure they would agree,
Betwixt their soules there is such sympathie.
  O where's your sweaty habite, when each Ape,
That can but spy the shadow of his shape,
That can no sooner ken what's vertuous,
But will auoyd it, and be vicious.
Without much doe, or farre fetch'd habiture
  In earnest thus, *It is a sacred cure*
To salue the soules dread wounds; *Omnipotent*
That Nature is, that cures the impotent,
Euen in a moment; *Sure Grace is infus'd*
By diuine fauour, not by actions vs'd.
Which is as perminent as heauens blisse
To them that haue it, then no habite is.
To morrow, nay, to day, it may be got:
So please that gracious Power clense thy spot.
  Vice, from priuation of that sacred Grace,
which God with-drawes, but puts not vice in place,
                    Who

CRAS.

Who sayes the sunne is cause of vgly night?
Yet when he vailes our eyes from his faire sight,
The gloomy curtaine of the night is spred.
Yee curious sotts, vainly by Nature led,
Where is your vice or vertuous habite now?
For *Sustine pro nunc* doth bend his brow,
And old crabb'd *Scotus* on th'organon
Pay'th me with snaphaunce, quick distinction,
Habites that intellectuall termed be,
Are got, or else infus'd from Deitie.
Dull Sorbonist, flie contradiction.
Fie, thou oppugn'st the definition.
If one should say, *Of things term'd rationall,*
Some reason haue, others meere sensuall.
Would not some freshman reading *Porphirie,*
Hisse, and deride such blockish foolerie?
Then vice nor vertue haue from habite place,
The one from want, the other sacred grace.

Infus'd

44

CRAS.

Infus'd, displac'd, not in our will or force,
But as it please Iehoua *haue remorce.*
I will, cries *Zeno,* ô presumption!
I can, thou maist, dogged oppinion
Of thwarting Cynicks. To day vicious,
List to their precepts, next day vertuous.
Peace *Seneca,* thou belchest blasphemy.
To liue from God, but to liue happily
(I heare thee boast,) *from thy Philosophy,*
And from thy selfe, ô rauening lunacy!
Cynicks, yee wound your selues, for Desteny
Ineuitable Fate, Necessity,
You hold doth sway the acts spirituall,
As well as parts of that we mortall call,
Wher's then (*I will?*) vvher's that strong Deity,
You doe ascribe to your Philosophy?
Confounded Natures brats, can *will* and *Fate,*
Haue both their seate, & office in your pate?

O

CRAS.

O hidden depth of that dread Secrecie,
Which I doe trembling touch in poetrie!
To day, to day, implore obsequiously,
Trust not *to morrowes will*, least vtterly
Yee be attach'd with sad confusion,
In your Grace-tempting lewd presumption.
    But I forget; why sweat I out my braine,
In deepe designes, to gay boyes lewd, and vaine?
These notes were better sung, mong better sort,
But to my pamphlet, few saue fooles resort.

Libri primi, finis.

S A-

SATY:
Liber secundus.

Proemium in librum secundum.

I Cannot quote a mott Italionate.
  Or brand my Satyres with som Spanish terme.
I cannot with swolne lines magnificate,
  Mine owne poore worth, or as immaculate
  Task others rimes, as if no blot did staine,
  No blemish soyle, my young Satyrick vaine.

Nor can I make my soule a merchandize,
  Seeking conceits to sute these Artlesse times.
Ordaine for base reward to poetize:
Soothing the vvorld, with oylie flatteries.
  Shall mercenary thoughts prouoke me write?
  Shall I for lucre be a Parasite?

Shall I once pen for vulgar sorts applause?
  To please each hound? each dungie Scauenger?
To fit some Oyster-wenches yawning iawes?
With tricksey tales of speaking Cornish dawes?
                                        First

Proemium in librum secundum.

First let my braine (bright hair'd *Latonas* sonne)
Be cleane distract with all confusion.

VVhat though some *Iohn-à-stile* will basely toyle,
  Onely incited with the hope of gaine,   (Moile
Though roguie thoughts doe force some iade-lyke
Yet no such filth my true-borne Muse will soyle.
  O *Epictetus*, I doe honour thee,
  To thinke how rich thou wert in pouertie.

Ad Rithmum.

COme pretty pleasing symphonie of words,
  Yee wel-match'd twins (whose like-tun'd tongs
Such musicall delight,) come willingly   (affords
And daunce *Leuoltoes* in my poesie.
                                        Come

Ad Rithmum.

Come all as easie, as spruce *Curio* vvill,
In some court hall to showe his capring skill.
As willingly come meete & iumpe together,
As new ioyn'd loues, when they do clip each other.
As willingly, as vvenches trip a round,
About a May-pole, after bagpipes sound.
Come riming numbers, come and grace conceite,
Adding a pleasing close, with your deceit
Inticing eares. Let not my ruder hand
Seeme once to force you in my lines to stand,
Be not so fearefull (pretty soules) to meete,
As *Flaccus* is the Sergiants face to greete.
Be not so backward loth to grace my sence,
As *Drusus* is, to haue intelligence
His Dad's aliue; but come into my head
As iocondly, as (when his wife was dead)
Young *Lelius* to his home. Come like-fac'd rime,
In tunefull numbers keeping musicks time.

But

Ad Rithmum.

But if you hange an arse, like *Tubered*,
When *Chremes* dragg'd him from his brothell bed,
Then hence base ballad stuffe, my poetry
Disclaimes you quite, for know my libertie
Scornes riming lawes; Alas poore idle sound,
Since I first *Phœbus* knew, I neuer found
Thy interest in sacred poesie.
Thou to Invention add'st but surquedry,
A gaudie ornature, but hast no part,
In that soule-pleasing high infused art.
Then if thou wilt clip kindly in my lines,
Welcome thou friendly ayde of my designes.
If not? No title of my sencelesse change
To wrest some forced rime, but freely range.
   Yee scrupulous obseruers, goe & learne
   Of *Æsops* dogge; meate from a shade discerne.

S A-

SATYRE. V.

♂ ☿

Totum in toto.

But if you hange a arse, like Tubered,
When Chremes doth complaine him his brothell bed,
Then hence base ballad stuffe, my poetry
Since I first Phædria neuer found
Thy

HAnge thy selfe *Drusus*, hast nor arms nor brain?
Some Sophy say, *The Gods sell all for paine*.
 Not so.
Had not that toyling Thebans steled back
Dread poysned shafts, liu'd he now, he should lack.
Spight of his farming Oxe-staules. *Themis* selfe
Would be casheir'd from one poore scrap of pelfe.
If that she were incarnate in our time
Shee might luske scorned in disdained slime,
Shaded from honour by some enuious mist
Of vvatry fogges, that fill the ill-stuft list
Of faire Desert, ielous euen of blind darke,
Least it should spie, and at theyr lamenes barke.
Honors shade, thrusts honours substance frõ his place.
Tis strange, when shade the substance can disgrace.
                                                    Harsh

Totum in toto.

Harsh lines cries *Curus*, whose eares nere reioyce
But at the quauering of my Ladies voyce.
Rude limping lines fits this lewd halting age,
Sweet senting *Curus*, pardon then my rage,
When wisards sweare plaine vertue neuer thriues,
None but *Priapus* by plaine dealing wiues.
Thou subtile *Hermes*, are the Destinies
Enamor'd on thee? then vp mount the skies.
Aduance, depose, doe euen what thou list,
So long as Fates doe grace thy iugling fist.
Tuscus, hast *Beuclarkes* armes and strong sinewes,
Large reach, full fed vaines, ample reuenewes?
Then make thy markets by thy proper arme,
O, brawny strength is an all-canning charme!
Thou dreadlesse *Thracian*, hast *Hallirrhotius* slaine?
What? ist not possible thy cause maintaine
Before the dozen *Areopagites?*
Come *Enagonian*, furnish him with slights.

             E.   Tut

Totum in Toto.

Tut, *Plutos* wrath, *Proserpina* can melt,
So that thy sacrifice be freely felt.
What cannot *Iuno* force in bed with *Ioue*?
Turne and returne a sentence with her loue.
Thou art too dusky. Fie thou shallow Asse,
Put on more eyes, and marke me as I passe.
Well plainly thus, *Sleight, Force, are mighty things,*
From which, much, (if not most) earths glory springs.
If Vertues selfe, were clad in humane shape,
Vertue without these, might goe beg and scrape.
The naked truth is, a well clothed lie,
A nimble quick-pate mounts to dignitie.
By force or fraude that matters not a iot,
So massie wealth may fall vnto thy lot.

   I heard old *Albius* sweare, *Flavus* should haue
His eldest gurle, for *Flavus* was a knaue.
A damn'd deep-reaching villaine, & would mount
He durst well warrant him to great account.
                                        What

54

Totum in toto.

What though he laid forth all his stock & store
Vpon some office, yet he'le gaine much more,
Though purchast deere. Tut, he will trebble it
In some few termes, by his extorting wit.
    When I in simple meaning went to sewe
For tong-tide *Damus*, that would needs goe wooe,
I praysd him for his vertue, honest life,
By God, cryes *Flora*, Ile not be his wife.
He'le nere come on. Now I sweare solemnly,
When I goe next, I'le praise his villany.
A better field to range in now a dayes,
If vice be vertue, I can all men prayse.
    What though pale *Maurus* paid huge symonies
For his halfe-dozen gelded vicaries.
Yet with good honest cut-throate vsury,
I feare he'le mount to reuerent dignity.
O sleight! all-canning sleight! all-damning sleight!
The onely gally-ladder vnto might.

E 2   *Tuscus*

Totum in Toto.

Tuscus is trade falne, yet great hope he'le rise,
For now he makes no count of periuries.
Hath drawne false lights from pitch-black loueries,
Glased his braided ware. Cogs, sweares, and lies,
Now since he hath the grace, thus gracelesse be
His neighbors sweare, he'le swell with treasurie.
Tut who maintaines, such goods ill got, decay.
No, they'le stick by thy soule, they'le nere away.
Luscus my Lords perfumer had no sale
Vntill he made his wife a brothell stale.
Absurd, the gods sell all for industry?
When, what's not got by hell-bred villany?
    Codrus my well-fac'd Ladies taile-bearer,
(He that some-times play'th *Flauias* vsherer)
I heard one day complaine to *Linceus*,
How vigilant, how right obsequious
Modest in carriage, how true in trust,
And yet (alas) nere guerdond with a crust.

But

Totum in toto.

But now I see, he findes by his accounts
That sole Priapus *by plaine dealing mounts.*
How now? what droupes the new *Pegasian* Inne?
I feare mine host is honest. Tut, beginne
To set vp whore-house. Nere too late to thriue
By any meanes at *Porta Rich*'ariue;
Goe vse some sleight, or liue poore *Irus* life,
Straight prostitute thy daughter, or thy wife.
And soone be wealthy, but be damn'd with it,
Hath not rich *Mylo* then deepe reaching wit?

          Faire age!
When tis a high, and hard thing t'haue repute
Of a compleat villaine, perfect, absolute,
And roguing vertue brings a man defame.
A packstaffe Epethite, and scorned name.
  Fie how my wit flaggs, how heauily
Me thinks I vent dull sprightlesse poesie.

Totum in toto.

What cold black frost congeales my nũmed brain?
What enuious power stops a Satyres vaine?
O now I know, the iugling God of sleights,
With *Caduceus* nimble *Hermes* fights,
And mists my wit. Offended that my rimes
Display his odious, world-abusing crimes.
  O be propitious, powerfull God of Arts,
I sheathe my weapons, and doe breake my darts,
Be then appeas'd, I'le offer to thy shrine,
An *Heccatombe*, of many spotted kine.
Myriades of beasts shall satisfie thy rage,
Which doe prophane thee in this Apish age.
  Infectious blood, yee gouty humors quake
  Whilst my sharp Razor doth incision make.

S A-

SATYRE. VI.

Hem nosti'n.

CVrio, know'st me? vvhy thou bottle-ale,
  Thou barmy froth! O stay me, least I raile
  Beyond *Nil vltra*, to see this butterfly,
  This windy bubble taske my balladry
With sencelesse censure. *Curio*, know'st my spright?
Yet deem'st that in sad seriousnes I write
Such nasty stuffe as is *Pigmalion?*
Such maggot-tainted lewd corruption?
  Ha, now he glauers with his fawning snowt,
And swears, he thought, I meant but faintly flowt,
My fine smug rime. O barbarous dropsie noule!
Think'st thou that *Genius* that attends my soule,
And guides my fist to scourge *Magnificoes*
Wil daigne my mind be ranck'd in *Paphian* showes?
Think'st thou, that I, which was create to whip
Incarnate fiends, will once vouchsafe to trip

A

Hem nosti'n.

A Paunis trauerse? or will lispe (*sweet loue*)
Or pule (*Aye me*) some female soule to moue?
Think'st thou, that I in melting poesie
Will pamper itching sensualitie?
(*That in the bodies scumme all fatally*
Intombes the soules most sacred facultie.)
   Hence thou misiudging Censor, know I wrot
Those idle rimes to note the odious spot
And blemish that deformes the lineaments
Of moderne Poesies habiliments.
Oh that the beauties of Invention,
For want of Iudgements disposition
Should all be soyl'd, ô that such treasurie,
Such straines of well-conceited poesie,
Should moulded be, in such a shapelesse forme,
That want of Art, should make such wit a scorne.
   Here's one must invocate some lose-legd Dame,
Some brothel drab, to helpe him stanzaes frame,
                          Or

Hem nosti'n.

Or els (alas) his wits can haue no vent
To broch conceits industrious intent.
Another yet dares tremblingly come out,
But first he must invoke good *Colin Clout*.
    Yon's one hath yean'd a fearefull prodigie,
Some monstrous mishapen Balladry,
His guts are in his braines, huge Iobbernoule,
Right Gurnets-head, the rest without all soule.
Another walkes, is lazie lies hym downe, (crowne
Thinkes, reades, at length some wonted sleep doth
His new falne lids, dreames, straight tenne pound to
Out steps some Fayery with quick motion, (one,
And tells him wonders, of some flowrie vale,
Awakes, straight rubs his eyes, and prints his tale.
    Yon's one, whose straines haue flowne so high a
That straight he flags, & tumbles in a ditch. (pitch
His sprightly hote high-soring poesie,
Is like that dreamed of Imagerie,
                       Whose

Hem nosti'n.

Whose head was golde, brest siluer, brassie thigh,
Lead leggs, clay feete; ô faire fram'd poesie.
    Here's one, to get an vndeseru'd repute
Of deepe deepe learning, all in fustian sute
Of ill-pac'd farre-fetch'd vvords attiereth
His period, that all sence forsweareth.
    Another makes old *Homer*, *Spencer* cite
Like my *Pigmalion*, where, with rage delight
He cryes, O *Ouid*. This causd my idle quill,
The worlds dull eares with such lewd stuffe to fill,
And gull vvith bumbast lines, the witlesse sence
Of these odde naggs; vvhose pates circumference
Is fild with froth! O these same buzzing Gnats
That sting my sleeping browes, these Nilus Rats,
Halfe dung, that haue theyr life from putrid slime.
These that doe prayse my loose lasciuious rime;
For these same shades, I seriously protest
I slubber'd vp that Chaos indigest,

                    To

Hem nosti'n.

To fish for fooles, that stalke in goodly shape,
What though in veluet cloake, yet still an Ape.
Capro reads, sweares, scrubs, and sweares againe,
Now by my soule an admirable straine,
Strokes vp his hayre, cries passing passing good,
Oh, there's a line incends his lustfull blood.
   Then *Muto* comes, with his new glasse-set face,
And with his late kist-hand my booke doth grace,
Straight reades, then smyles, & lisps (*tis pretty good*)
And praiseth that he neuer vnderstood.
But roome for *Flaccus*, he'le my Satyres read.
Oh how I trembled straight with inward dread!
But when I saw him read my fustian,
And head him sweare I was a Pythian,
Yet straight recald, & sweares I did but quote
Out of *Xilinum* to that margents note,
I could scarce hold, and keepe my selfe conceal'd,
But had well-nigh my selfe and all reueal'd.
                                        Then

63

Hem nosti'n.

Then straight comes *Friscus*, that neat gentleman
That newe discarded Academien,
Who for he could cry (*Ergo*) in the schoole,
Straight-way, with his huge iudgement dares con-
Whatso'ere he viewes, *that's prety, prety good*, (trole
That Epithete hath not that sprightly blood
Which should enforce it speake, that's Persius *vaine*,
That's Iuvenals, *heere*'s Horace *crabbed straine*,
Though he nere read one line in *Iuvenall*,
Or in his life his lazie eye let fall
On duskie *Persius*. O indignitie
To my respectlesse free-bred poesie.

Hence ye big-buzzing little-bodied Gnats,
Yee tatling Ecchoes, huge tongu'd pigmy brats,
I meane to sleepe, wake not my slumbring braine
With your malignant weake detracting vaine.

What though the sacred issue of my soule
I heare expose to Ideots controule?

What

Hem nosti'n.

What though I bare to lewd Opinion
Lay ope to vulgar prophanation
My very *Genius.* Yet know my poesie
Doth scorne your vtmost, ranck'st indignitie.
  My pate was great with child, & here tis eas'd,
  Vexe all the world, so that thy selfe be pleas'd.

SATYRE. VII.

A Cynicke Satyre.

A *Man, a man, a kingdome for a man.*
  Why how now currish mad Athenian?
Thou Cynick dogge, see'st not streets do swarme
With troupes of men? No, no, for *Circes* charme
Hath turn'd them all to Swine; I neuer shall
Thinke those same *Samian* sawes authenticall,
                                        But

A Cynicke Satyre.

But rather I dare sweare, the soules of swine
Doe liue in men, for that same radiant shine,
That lustre wherewith natures *Nature* decked
Our intellectuall part, that glosse is soyled
With stayning spots of vile impietie,
And muddy durt of sensualitie,
These are no men, but *Apparitions*,
Ignes fatui, Glowormes, Fictions,
Meteors, Ratts of Nilus, Fantasies,
Colosses, Pictures, Shades, Resemblances.

Ho *Linceus!*
Seest thou yon gallant in the sumptuous clothes,
How brisk, how spruce, how gorgiously he showes,
Note his French-herring bones, but note no more,
Vnlesse thou spy his fayre appendant whore
That lackyes him. Marke nothing but his clothes,
His new stampt complement, his Cannon oathes.
Marke

A Cynicke Satyre.

Marke those, for naught but such lewd viciousnes
Ere graced him, saue Sodome beastlines.
Is this a *Man?* Nay, an incarnate deuill,
That struts in vice, and glorieth in euill.
   A man, a man, peace Cynick, yon is one,
A compleat soule, of all perfection.
What, mean'st thou him that walks al opẽ brested?
Drawne through the eare with Ribands,plumy cre-
He that doth snort in fat-fed luxury,   (sted?
And gapes for some grinding Monopoly?
He that in effeminate inuention,
In beastly source of all pollution,
In ryot, lust, and fleshly seeming sweetnes,
Sleepes sound secure, vnder the shade of greatnes?
Mean'st, thou that sencelesse, sensuall Epicure?
That sincke of filth, that guzzell most impure?
What he? *Linceus* on my word thus presume,
He's nought but clothes, & senting sweet perfume.
                      His

A Cynicke Satyre.

His very soule, assure thee *Linceus*,
Is not so big as is an Atomus:
Nay, he is sprightlesse, sence or soule hath none,
Since last *Medusa* turn'd him to a stone.
    A man, a man, Loe yonder I espie
The shade of *Nestor* in sad grauitie;
Since old *Sylenus* brake his Asses back,
He now is forc'd his paunch, and guts to pack
In a faire Tumbrell. Why sower Satirist
Canst thou vnman him? Here I dare insist
And soothly say, he is a perfect soule,
Eates Nectar, drinks Ambrosia, saunce controule,
An invndation of felicity
Fats him with honor, and huge treasury.
Canst thou not *Linceus* cast thy searching eye
And spy his immynent Catastrophe?
He's but a spunge, and shortly needs must leese
His wrong got iuice, when greatnes fist shal squeese
                  His

A Cynicke Satyre.

His liquor out. Would not some shallow head,
That is with seeming shadowes onely fed,
Sweare yon same Damaske-coat, yon garded man,
Were some graue sober *Cato Vtican?*
When let him but in iudgments sight vncase,
He's naught but budge, old gards, browne foxe-fur
He hath no soule, the which the Stagerite   (face
Term'd rationall, for beastly appetite.
Base dunghill thoughts, and sensuall action,
Hath made him loose that faire creation.
And now no man, since *Circes* magick charme
Hath turn'd him to a maggot, that doth swarme
In tainted flesh, whose foule corruption
Is his faire foode, whose generation
Anothers ruine. O *Canaans* dread curse
To liue in peoples sinnes. Nay farre more worse
To muck ranke hate. But sirra, *Linceus,*
Seest thou that troope that now affronteth vs?
F.   They

A Cynicke Satyre.

They are naught but Eeles, that neuer will appeare,
Till that tempestuous winds or thunder teare
Their slimy beds. But prithee stay a while,
Looke, yon comes *Iohn-a-noke*, and *Iohn-a-stile*,
They are naught but slow-pac'd, dilatory pleas,
Demure demurrers, still striuing to appease
Hote zealous loue. The language that they speake,
Is the pure barbarous blacksaunt of the *Geate*,
Their onely skill rests in *Collusions*,
Abatements, *stopples*, *inhibitions*.
Heauy-pac'd Iades, dull pated Iobernoules,
Quick in delayes, checking with vaine controules
Faire Iustice course, vile necessary euils,
Smooth seeme-Saints,yet damn'd incarnate deuils.
  Farre be it from my sharpe Satirick Muse,
Those graue, and reuerent legists to abuse,
That ayde *Astrea*, that doe further right:
But these *Megera's* that inflame despight,

That

A Cynicke Satyre.

That broch deepe ranchor, that doe study still
To ruine right, that they their panch may fill
With *Irus* blood; these Furies I doe mean,
These Hedge-hogs, that disturbe *Astreas* Scean.
  A man, a man: peace Cynick, yon's a man,
Behold yon sprightly dread *Mauortian*.
With him I stop thy currish barking chops.
what? meanst thou him, that in his swaggering slops
Wallowes vnbraced all along the streete?
He that salutes each gallant he doth meete,
With *farewell sweet Captaine, kind hart, adew*,
He that last night, tumbling thou didst view
From out the great mans head, and thinking still
He had beene Sentinell of vvarlike Brill.
Cryes out *Que va la?* zownds *Que?* and out doth
His transformd ponyard, to a *Syrrenge* straw, (draw
And stabs the Drawer. What that *Ringo roote?*
Mean'st thou that wasted leg, puffe bumbast boote?

What

A Cynicke Satyre.

What he that's drawne, and quartered with lace?
That *Wespalian* gamon Cloue-stuck face?
Why, he is naught but huge blaspheming othes,
Swart snowt, big looks, mishapen Swizers clothes,
Weake meager lust hath now consumed quite,
And wasted cleane away his martiall spright,
Infeebling ryot, all vices confluence,
Hath eaten out that sacred influence
VVhich made him man.
That diuine part is soak'd away in sinne,
In sensuall lust, and midnight bezeling.
Ranke invndation of luxuriousnes,
Haue tainted him with such grosse beastlines,
That now the seate of that celestiall essence
Is all possest with Naples pestilence.
Fat peace, and dissolute impiety,
Haue lulled him in such security,

That

A Cynicke Satyre.

That now, let whirlwinds and confusion teare
The Center of our state, let Giants reare
Hill vpon hill, let vvesterne *Termagant*
Shake heauens vault, he with his Occupant,
Are cling'd so close, like dew-wormes in the morne,
That he'le not stir, till out his guts are torne
With eating filth. *Tubrio* snort on, snort on,
Till thou art wak'd with sad confusion.
    Now raile no more at my sharpe Cynick sound
Thou brutish world, that in all vilenes drown'd
Hast lost thy soule, for naught but shades I see,
Resemblances of men inhabite thee.
    Yon Tissue slop, yon Holy-crossed pane,
Is but a vvater-spaniell that will faune
And kisse the water whilst it pleasures him,
But being once arriued at the brim,
He shakes it off.

F 3   Yon

A Cynicke Satyre.

Yon in the capring cloake, a Mimick Ape
That onely striues to seeme an others shape.
  Yon's *Æsops* Asse, yon sad ciuility,
Is but an Oxe, that with base drudgery
Eares vp the Land, whilst some gilt Asse doth chaw
The golden wheat; he well apay'd with straw.
  Yon's but a muckhill ouer-spred with snow,
Which with that vaile doth euen as fairely show
As the greene meades, whose natiue outward faire
Breathes sweet perfumes into the neighbour ayre.
  Yon effeminate sanguine *Ganimede*,
Is but a Beuer, hunted for the bed.
  Peace Cynick, *see what yonder doth approach,*
A cart? a tumbrell? *no a Badged coach.*
What's in't? some man. *No, nor yet woman kinde,*
But a celestiall Angell, faire refinde.
The deuill as soone. Her maske so hinders me
I cannot see her beauties deitie.

Now

A Cynicke Satyre.

Now that is off, shee is so vizarded,
So steep'd in Lemons iuyce, so surphuled
I cannot see her face, vnder one hood
Two faces, but I neuer vnderstood
Or saw, one face vnder two hoods till now,
Tis the right semblance of old *Ianus* brow.
   Her maske, her vizard, her loose-hanging gowne
For her loose lying body, her bright spãgled crown,
Her long slit sleeue, stiffe, buske, puffe verdingall,
Is all that makes her thus angelicall.
Alas, her soule struts round about her neck,
Her seate of sence is her rebato set,
Her intellectuall is a fained nicenes,
Nothing but clothes, & simpering precisenes.
   Out on these puppets, painted Images,
Haberdashers shops, torch-light maskeries, (bright
Perfuming pans, Duch antients, Glowe-vvormes
That soile our soules, and dampe our reasons light:
                     Away,

A Cynicke Satyre.

Away, away, hence Coach-man, goe inshrine
Thy new glas'd puppet in port Esqueline.
Blush *Martia*, feare not, or looke pale, all's one,
Margara keepes thy set complexion.
Sure I nere think those axioms to be true,
That soules of men, from that great soule ensue,
And of his essence doe participate
As't were by pipes, when so degenerate,
So aduerse is our natures motion,
To his immaculate condition:
That such foule filth, from such faire purity,
Such sensuall acts from such a Deity,
Can nere proceed. But if that dreame were so,
Then sure the slime that from our soules doe flow,
Haue stopt those pipes by which it was conuai'd,
And now no humane creatures, once disrai'd
Of that faire iem.
Beasts *sence*, plants *growth*, like being as a stone,
But out alas, our *Cognisance* is gone.
            Finis libri Secundi.

SATY:
Liber Tertius.

Proemium in librum tertium.

IN serius iest, and iesting seriousnes,
I striue to scourge poluting beastlines.
I invocate no *Delian* Deitie,
Nor sacred of-spring of *Mnemosyne*:
I pray in ayde of no *Castalian* Muse,
No Nimph, no femall Angell to infuse
A sprightly wit to raise my flagging wings,
And teach me tune these harsh discordant strings;
I craue no Syrens of our Halcion times,
To grace the accents of my rough-hew'd rimes;
But grim *Reproofe*, stearne Hate of villany,
Inspire and guide a Satyres poesie.
Faire *Detestation* of foule odious sinne,
In which our swinish times lye wallowing.

Be

Proemium in librum tertium.

Be thou my conduct and my *Genius*,
My wits inciting sweet breath'd *Zephirus*.
O that a Satyres hand had force to plucke
Some fludgate vp, to purge the world from muck:
Would God I could turne *Alpheus* riuer in
To purge this *Augean* oxstaule from foule sin.
 Well, I will try, awake impuritie,
  And view the vaile drawne from thy villanie.

Inamo-

SATYRE. VIII.

Inamorato Curio.

CVrio, aye mee! thy mistres Monkey's dead,
   Alas, alas, her pleasures buried.
   Goe womans slaue, performe his exequies,
Condole his death in mournfull Elegies.
Tut, rather Peans sing *Hermaphrodite*,
For that sad death giues life to thy delight.
  Sweet fac'd *Corinna*, daine the riband tie
Of thy Cork-shooe, or els thy slaue will die:
Some puling Sonnet toles his passing bell,
Some sighing Elegie must ring his knell,
Vnlesse bright sunshine of thy grace reuiue
His wambling stomack, certes he will diue
Into the whirle-poole of deuouring death,
And to some Mermaid sacrifice his breath.
Then oh, *oh then*, to thy eternall shame,
And to the honour of sweet *Curios* name,

                       This

Inamorato Curio.

This Epitaph vpon the Marble stone,
Must fayre be grau'd of that true louing one;
 Heere lyeth hee, hee lyeth heere,
  that bounc'd, and pitty cried,
 The doore not op'd, fell sicke alas,
  alas fell sicke and dyed.
What Mirmidon, or hard Dolopian,
What sauage minded rude Cyclopian,
But such a sweete pathetique Paphian
Would force to laughter? Ho *Amphitrion*,
Thou art no Cuckold, what though *Ioue* dallied
During thy warres, in faire *Alcmenas* bed,
Yet *Hercules* true borne, that imbecilitie
Of corrupt nature all apparantly
Appeares in him, ô foule indignitie,
I heard him vow himselfe a slaue to *Omphale*,
Puling (*aye me*) ô valours obloquie!
He that the inmost nookes of hell did know,
Whose nere craz'd prowesse all did ouer-throw,

Inamorato Curio.

Lyes streaking brawnie limmes in weakning bed,
Perfum'd, smooth kemb'd, new glaz'd, faire surphu-
O that the boundlesse power of the soule   (led,
Should be subiected to such base controule!

  Big limm'd *Alcides*, doffe thy honors crowne,
Goe spin huge slaue, least *Omphale* should frowne.
By my best hopes, I blush with griefe and shame
To broach the peasant basenes of our name.

  O now my ruder hand begins to quake,
To thinke what loftie Cedars I must shake:
But if the canker fret the barkes of Oakes,
Like humbler shrubs shall equall beare the stroakes
Of my respectlesse rude Satyrick hand,

  Vnlesse the Destin's adamantine band
Should tye my teeth, I cannot chuse but bite,
To view *Mauortius* metamorphiz'd quite
To puling sighes, & into (*aye mee's*) state,
With voyce distinct, all fine articulate.

Lisping

Inamorato Curio.

Lisping, *Faire saint, my woe compassionate,*
By heauen thine eye is my soule-guiding fate.
   The God of wounds, had wont on *Cyprian* couch
To streake himselfe, and with incensing touch
To faint his force onely when wrath had end;
But now, mong furious garboiles, he doth spend
His feebled valour, in tilt and turneing,
With wet turn'd kisses, melting dallying.
A poxe apon't, that *Bacchis* name should be
The watch-word giuen to the souldierie.
Goe troupe to fielde, mount thy obscured fame,
Cry out S. *George*, invoke thy Mistres name;
Thy Mistres and S. *George*, alarum cry,
Weake force, weake ayde, that sproutes from luxurie.
   Thou tedious workmanship of lust-stung *Ioue*
Downe from thy skies, enioy our females loue,
Some fiftie more *Beotian* gerles will sue
To haue thy loue, (so that thy backe be true.)

O

Inamorato Curio.

O now me thinks I heare swart *Martius* cry
Souping along in warrs fain'd maskerie,
By *Lais* starrie front he'le forth-with die
In cluttred blood, his Mistres liuorie.
Her fancies colours waues vpon his head,
O well fenc'd *Albion*, mainly manly sped,
When those that are Soldadoes in thy state,
Doe beare the badge of base, effeminate,
Euen on their plumie crests, brutes sensuall,
Hauing no sparke of intellectuall.
Alack, what hope? when some ranck nasty wench
Is subiect of theyr vowes and confidence?
  Publius hates vainely to idolatries,
And laughs that Papists honour Images,
And yet (ô madnes) these mine eyes did see
Him melt in mouing plaints, obsequiously
Imploring fauour, twining his kinde armes,
Vsing inchauntments, exorcismes, charmes.
                                        The

Inamorato Curio.

The oyle of Sonnets, wanton blandishment,
The force of teares, & seeming languishment,
Vnto the picture of a painted lasse:
I saw him court his Mistres looking-glasse,
Worship a busk-poynt, (which in secrecie
I feare was conscius of strange villany.)
I saw him crouch, deuote his liuelihood,
Sweare, protest, vow pesant seruitude
Vnto a painted puppet, to her eyes
I heard him sweare his sighs to sacrifice.
But if he get her itch-allaying pinne,
O sacred relique, straight he must beginne
To raue out-right, then thus. *Celestiall blisse,*
Can heauen grant so rich a grace as this?
Touch it not (by the Lord Sir) tis diuine,
It once beheld her radiant eyes bright shine:
Her haire imbrac'd it, ô thrice happy prick
That there was thron'd, and in her haire didst stick.
  G.   Kisse,

Inamorato Curio.

Kisse, blesse, adore it *Publius*, neuer linne,
Some sacred vertue lurketh in the pinne.
   O frantick fond pathetique passion!
Ist possible such sensuall action
Should clip the wings of contemplation?
O can it be the spirits function,
The soule not subiect to dimension,
Should be made slaue to reprehension
Of crafty natures paint? Fie, can our soule
Be vnderling to such a vile controule?
   Saturio wish'd himselfe his Mistres buske,
That he might sweetly lie, and softly luske
Betweene her paps, then must he haue an eye
At eyther end, that freely might discry
Both hils and dales. But out on *Phrigio*,
That wish'd he were his Mistris dog, to goe
And licke her milk-white fist, ô pretty grace,
That pretty *Phrigio* begs but Pretties place.

Par-

Inamorato Curio.

Parthenophell, thy wish I will omit,
So beastly tis I may not vtter it.
But *Punicus*, of all I'le beare with thee,
That faine would'st be thy Mistres smug Munkey,
Here's one would be a flea, (iest comicall)
Another his sweet Ladies verdingall
To clip her tender breech; Another he
Her siluer-handled fanne would gladly be,
Here's one would be his Mistres neck-lace faine,
To clip her faire, and kisse her azure vaine.
Fond fooles, well wish'd, and pitty but should be,
For beastly shape to brutish soules agree.
  If *Lauras* painted lip doe daine a kisse
To her enamor'd slaue, *ô heauens blisse*
(Straight he exclaimes) *not to be match'd with this!*
Blaspheming dolt, goe three-score sonnets write
Vpon a pictures kisse, ô rauing spright!

G 2   I

Inamorato Curio.

I am not saplesse, old, or rumatick,
No *Hipponax* mishapen stigmatick,
That I should thus inueigh gainst amorous spright
Of him whose soule doth turne *Hermaphrodite*,
But I doe sadly grieue, and inly vexe
To view the base dishonors of our sexe.　(rapes,
　　Tush, guiltles Doues, when Gods to force foule
Will turne themselues to any brutish shapes.
Base bastard powers, whom the world doth see
Transform'd to swine for sensuall luxurie;
The sonne of *Saturne* is become a Bull,
To crop the beauties of some female trull.
Now, when he hath his first wife *Metim* sped,
And fairely chok'd, least foole gods should be bred
Of that fond Mule, *Themis* his second wife
Hath turn'd away, that his vnbrideled life
Might haue more scope.　Yet last his sisters loue
Must satiate the lustfull thoughts of *Ioue*.

　　　　　　　　　　　　　　　Now

Inamorato Curio.

Now doth the lecher in a Cuckowes shape
Commit a monstrous and incestuous rape.
Thrice sacred gods, and ô thrice blessed skies
Whose orbes includes such vertuous deities!
    What should I say? Lust hath confounded all,
The bright glosse of our intellectuall
Is fouly soyl'd. The wantōn wallowing
In fond delights, and amorous dallying,
Hath dusk'd the fairest splendour of our soule:
Nothing now left, but carkas, lothsome, foule.
For sure, if that some spright remained still,
Could it be subiect to lewd *Lais* will?
    Reason by prudence in her function
Had wont to tutor all our action
Ayding with precepts of philosophy
Our feebled natures imbecility:
But now affection, will, concupiscence,
Haue got o're Reason chiefe preheminence.

G 3

Tis

Inamorato Curio.

Tis so, els how, should such basenes taint
As force it be made slaue to natures paint?
Me thinks the spirits Pegase *Fantasie*
Should hoise the soule from such base slauery,
But now I see, and can right plainly show
Frõ whence such abiect thoughts & actions grow.
  Our aduerse body, being earthly, cold,
Heauy, dull, mortall, would not long infold
A stranger inmate, that was backward still
To all his dungy, brutish, sensuall will:
Now here-vpon, our Intellectuall,
Compact of fire all celestiall,
Invisible, immortall, and diuine,
Grew straight to scorn his land-lords muddy slime.
And therfore now is closely slunke away
(Leauing his smoaky house of mortall clay)
Adorn'd with all his beauties liniaments
And brightest iems of shining ornaments.
                   His

Inamorato Curio.

His parts diuine, sacred, spirituall
Attending on him, leauing the sensuall
Base hangers on, lusking at home in slime,
Such as wont to stop port Esqueline.
Now doth the body led with sencelesse will,
(The which in reasons absence ruleth still)
Raue, talke idely, as'twere some deity
Adoring female painted puppetry
Playing at put-pin, doting on some glasse
(Which breath'd but on his falsed glosse doth passe)
Toying with babies, and with fond pastime
Some childrens sport, deflowring of chast time,
Imploying all his wits in vaine expence,
Abusing all his organons of sence.
    Returne, returne, sacred *Synderesis*,
Inspire our truncks, let not such mud as this
Pollute vs still. Awake our lethargy,
Raise vs from out our brain-sicke foolery.

                                    S A-

❧ *Here's a toy to mocke an*

Ape indeede.

GRim-fac'd *Reproofe*, sparkle with threatning eye
Bend thy sower browes in my tart poesie.
Auant yee curres, houle in some cloudy mist,
Quake to behold a sharp-fang'd Satyrist.
O how on tiptoes proudly mounts my Muse,
Stalking a loftier gate then Satyres vse.
Me thinks some sacred rage warmes all my vaines,
Making my spright mount vp to higher straines
Then wel beseemes a rough-tongu'd Satyres part,
But Art curbs Nature, Nature guildeth Art.

Come downe yee Apes, or I will strip you quite,
Baring your bald tayles to the peoples sight
Yee Mimick slaues, what are you percht so hie?
Downe Iack an Apes from thy fain'd royaltie.
What furr'd with beard, cas'd in a Satin sute
Iudiciall Iack? how hast thou got repute

Of

A toy to mocke an Ape.

Of a sound censure? O ideot times,
Whẽ gawdy Monkeyes mowe ore sprightly rimes!
O world of fooles, when all mens iudgment's set
And rests vpon some mumping Marmoset!
   Yon Athens Ape (that can but simperingly
Yaule *auditores humanissimi*,
Bound to some seruile imitation,
Can with much sweat patch an Oration,)
Now vp he comes, and with his crooked eye
Presumes to squint on some faire Poesie;
And all as thanklesse as vngratefull Thames
He slinks away, leauing but reeching steames
Of dungy slime behind, all as ingrate
He vseth it, as when I satiate   (roome,
My spaniells paunch, vvho straight perfumes the
With his tailes filth: so this vnciuill groome,
Ill-tutor'd pedant, *Mortimers* numbers
With muck-pit esculine filth bescumbers.

                                        Now

93

A toy to mocke an Ape.

Now th' Ape chatters, and is as malecontent
As a bill-patch'd doore, vvhose entrailes out haue
And spewd theyr tenant.   (sent
　　My soule adores iudiciall schollership,
But when to seruile imitatorship
Some spruce Athenian pen is prentized,
Tis worse then Apish. Fie, be not flattered
With seeming worth, fond affectation
Befits an Ape, and mumping Babilon.

　　O what a tricksie lerned nicking straine
Is this applauded, sencles, modern *vaine
When late I heard it frō sage *Mutius* lips
How ill me thought such wanton Iigging skips
Beseem'd his grauer speech. *Farre flie thy fame*
Most, most, of me belou'd, whose silent name
One letter bounds. Thy true iudiciall stile
I euer honour, and if my loue beguile

Not

* Nō ledere,
sed ludere
non lanea,
sed linea
non ictus,
sed nictus
potius.

A toy to mocke an Ape.

Not much my hopes, then thy vnvalued worth
Shall mount faire place, when Apes are turned forth.
   I am too mild, reach me my scourge againe,
O yon's a pen speakes in a learned vaine.
Deepe, past all sence. Lanthorne & candle light,
Here's all invisible, *all mentall spright.*
What hotchpotch, giberidge, doth the Poet bring?
How strangely speakes? yet sweetly doth he sing.
I once did know a tinckling Pewterer,
That was the vildest stumbling stutterer
That euer hack'd and hew'd our natiue tongue,
Yet to the Lute if you had heard him sung,
Iesu how sweet he breath'd. You can apply.
O sencelesse prose, iudiciall poesie,
How ill you'r link'd: This affectation,
To speake beyond mens apprehension,
How Apish tis. When all in fusten sute
Is cloth'd a huge *nothing*, all for repute

Of

95

A toy to mocke an Ape.

Of profound knowledge, whẽ profoũdnes knowes
There's nought cõtaind, but only seeming showes.
   Old Iack of Parris-garden, canst thou get
A faire rich sute, though fouly runne in debt?
Looke smug, smell sweet, take vp commodities,
Keepe whores, fee baudes, belch impious blasphe-
Wallow along in swaggering disguise,   (mies,
Snuffe vp smoak whiffs, & each morne fore she rise
Visite thy drab? Canst vse a false cut Die
With a cleane grace, and glib facilitie?
Canst thunder cannon oathes, like th'ratling
Of a huge, double, full-charg'd culuering?
Then Iack troupe mong our gallants, kisse thy fist,
And call them brothers. Say a Satyrist
Sweares they are thine in neere affinitie.
All coosin germaines, saue in villanie.
For (sadly truth to say) what are they els
But imitators of lewd beastlines?

Farre

A toy to mocke an Ape.

Farre worse then Apes; for mowe, or scratch your
It may be some odde Ape will imitate.   (pate,
But let a youth that hath abus'd his time,
In wronged trauaile, in that hoter clime,
Swoope by old Iack, in clothes Italionate:
And I'le be hang'd if he will imitate
His strange fantastique sute shapes. ---
Or let him bring or'e beastly luxuries,
Some hell-deuised lustfull villanies,
Euẽ Apes & beasts wold blush with natiue shame,
And thinke it foule dishonour to theyr name,
Their beastly name, to imitate such sin
As our lewd youths doe boast and glory in.

    Fie, whether doe these Monkeys carry mee?
Theyr very names doe soyle my poesie.
Thou vvorld of Marmosets and mumping Apes,
Vnmaske, put of thy fained borrowed shapes.
                        Why

A toy to mocke an Ape.

Why lookes neate *Curus* all so simperingly?
Why babbles thou of deepe Diuinitie?
And of that sacred testimoniall?
Liuing voluptuous like a *Bacchanall?*
Good hath thy tongue: but thou ranke Puritan,
I'le make an Ape as good a Christian.
I'le force him chatter, turning vp his eye
Looke sad, goe graue. Demure ciuilitie
Shall seeme to say, *Good brother, sister deere,*
As for the rest, to snort in belly cheere,
To bite, to gnaw, and boldly intermell
VVith sacred things, in which thou doost excell,
Vnforc'd he'le doe. O take compassion
Euen on your soules, make not religion
A bawde to lewdnes. Ciuill *Socrates,*
Clip not the youth of *Alcebiades*
With vnchast armes. Disguised *Messaline,*
I'le teare thy maske, and bare thee to the eyne

Of

98

A toy to mocke an Ape.

Of hissing boyes, if to the Theaters
I finde thee once more come for lecherers
To satiate? Nay, to tyer thee with the vse
Of weakening lust. Yee fainers, leaue t'abuse
Our better thoughts with your hipocrisie,
Or by the euer-liuing Veritie,
I'le strip you nak'd, and whyp you with my rimes,
Causing your shame to liue to after times.

SATYRA NOVA.

Stultorum plena sunt omnia.

To his very friend, Maister E. G.

FRom out the sadnes of my discontent,
Hating my wonted iocund merriment,
(Onely to giue dull Time a swifter wing)
Thus scorning scorne of Ideot fooles, I sing.

I

99

Stultorum plena sunt omnia.

I dread no bending of an angry brow,
Or rage of fooles that I shall purchase now.
Who'le scorne to sitte in ranke of foolery
VVhen I'le be maister of the company?
For pre-thee *Ned*, I pre-thee gentle lad,
Is not he frantique, foolish, bedlam mad,
That wastes his spright, that melts his very braine
In deepe designes, in wits darke gloomie straine?
That scourgeth great slaues with a dreadlesse fist,
Playing the rough part of a Satyrist,
To be perus'd by all the dung-scum rable
Of thin-braind Ideots, dull, vncapable?
For mimicke apish schollers, pedants, gulls,
Perfum'd Inamoratoes, brothell trulls?
Whilst I (poore soule) abuse chast virgin Time,
Deflowring her with vnconceiued rime.
Tut, tut, a toy of an idle empty braine,
Some scurrill iests, light gew-gawes, fruitlesse, vaine.
                                              Cries

Stultorum plena sunt omnia.

Cryes beard-graue *Dromus*, whē alas, God knowes,
His toothles gums nere chaw but outward showes.
Poore Budgeface, bowcase sleeue, but let him passe,
Once fur and beard shall priuiledge an Asse.
   And tell me *Ned*, vvhat might that gallant be,
Who to obtaine intemperate luxurie,
Cuckolds his elder brother, gets an heire,
By which his hope is turned to dispaire?
In fayth, (good *Ned*) he damn'd himselfe with cost,
For well thou know'st full goodly land was lost.
   I am too priuate. *Yet mee thinkes an Asse,*
Rimes well with VIDERIT VTILITAS.
Euen full as well, I boldly dare auer
As any of that stinking Scauenger
Which from his dunghill hee bedaubed on
The latter page of old *Pigmalion.*
O that thys brother of hypocresie,
(Applauded by his pure fraternitie)
           H.   Should

Stultorum plena sunt omnia.

Should thus be puffed, and so proude insist,
As play on mee the Epigramatist.
Opinion mounts this froth vnto the skies,
Whom iudgements reason iustly vilefies.
For, (shame to the Poet,) reade *Ned*, behold
How wittily a Maisters-hoode can scold.

An Epigram which the Authour *Vergidemiarum*,
caused to bee pasted to the latter page of euery
Pigmalion that came to the stacioners of Cambridge.

J Ask'd Phisitions what theyr counsell was
  For a mad dogge, or for a mankind Asse?
They told mee though there were confections store,
Of Poppy-seede, and soueraine Hellebore,
The dog was best cured by cutting & * kinsing, * Mark the
The Asse must be kindly whipped for winsing. witty allu-
Nowe then S. K. I little passe sion to my
VVhether thou be a mad dog, or a mankind Asse. name.

                                              Smart

Stultorum plena sunt omnia.

Medice cura teipsum.

Smart ierke of vvit, did euer such a straine
Rise from an Apish schoole-boyes childish braine?
Doost thou not blush (good) *Ned*, that such a sent
Should rise frõ thence where thou hadst nutriment?
Shame to Opinion, that perfumes his dung,
And streweth flowers rotten bones among,
Iugling Opinion, thou inchaunting witch,
Paint not a rotten post with colours rich.
But now this Iugler with the worlds consent
Hath halfe his soule; the other, Compliment,
Mad world the whilst. But I forget mee I,
I am seduced with this poesie:
And madder then a Bedlam spend sweet time
In bitter numbers, in this idle rime,
Out on this humour. From a sickly bed,
And from a moodie minde distempered,

H 2

Stultorum plena sunt omnia.

I vomit foorth my loue, now turn'd to hate,
Scorning the honour of a Poets state.
Nor shall the kennell route of muddy braines,
Rauish my Muses heyre, or heare my straines
Once more. No nittie pedant shall correct
Ænigmaes to his shallow Intelect
Inchauntment. *Ned* hath rauished my sence
In a Poetick vaine circumference.
Yet thus I hope, (God shield I now should lie)
Many more fooles, and most more wise then I.

VALE.

SATYRE. X.

Humours.

SLeep grim *Reproofe*, my iocond Muse doth sing
In other keyes, to nimbler fingering.
Dull sprighted *Melancholy*, leaue my braine
To hell *Cimerian* night, in liuely vaine
I striue to paint, then hence all darke intent
And sullen frownes, come sporting meriment,
Cheeke dimpling laughter, crowne my very soule
With iouisance, whilst mirthfull iests controule
The goutie humours of these pride-swolne dayes,
Which I doe long vntill my pen displaies.
O I am great with mirth, some midwifrie,
Or I shall breake my sides at vanitie.
　　Roome for a capering mouth, whose lips nere
But in discoursing of the gracefull slur:　　(stur,
Who euer heard spruce skipping *Curio*
Ere prate of ought, but of the whirle on toe.

H 3　　　　　　　　The

The turne aboue ground, *Robrus* sprauling kicks,
Fabius caper, *Harries* tossing tricks?
Did euer any eare, ere heare him speake
Vnlesse his tongue of crosse-poynts did intreat?
His teeth doe caper whilst he eates his meate,
His heeles doe caper, whilst he takes his seate,
His very soule, his intellectuall
Is nothing but a mincing capreall.   (meete
He dreames of toe-turnes, each gallant hee dooth
He fronts him with a trauers in the streete,
Prayse but *Orchestra*, and the skipping art,
You shall commaund him, faith you haue his hart
Euen capring in your fist. A hall, a hall,
Roome for the Spheres, the Orbes celestiall
Will daunce *Kemps Iigge*. They'le reuel with neate
A worthy Poet hath put on their Pumps? (iumps
O wits quick trauers, but *sance ceo's* slow,
Good faith tis hard for nimble *Curio*.

Yee

Humours.

Yee gracious Orbes, keepe the old measuring,
All's spoyld if once yee fall to capering.

 Luscus what's playd to day? fayth now I know
I set thy lips abroach, from whence doth flow
Naught but pure *Iuliet* and *Romeo.*
Say, who acts best? *Drusus,* or *Roscio?*
Now I haue him, that nere of ought did speake
But when of playes or Plaiers he did treate.
H'ath made a common-place booke out of playes,
And speakes in print, at least what ere he sayes
Is warranted by Curtaine *plaudities,*
If ere you heard him courting *Lesbias* eyes;
Say (Curteous Sir) speakes he not mouingly
From out some new pathetique Tragedie?
He writes, he railes, he iests, he courts, what not,
And all from out his huge long scraped stock
Of well penn'd playes.

         Oh

Humours.

Oh come not within distance, *Martius* speakes,
Who nere discourseth but of fencing feates,
Of *counter times*, *finctures*, slye *passataes*,
Stramazones, resolute *Stoccataes*,
Of the quick change, with wiping *mandritta*,
The *carricado*, with th'*enbrocata*,
Oh, by *Iesu Sir*, (me thinks I heare him cry)
The honourable fencing misterie,
Who doth not honour? Then falls he in againe,
Iading our eares, and some-what must be saine
Of blades, and Rapier-hilts, of surest garde,
Of *Vincentio*, and the *Burgonians* ward.
Thys bumbast foile-button I once did see
By chaunce, in *Liuias* modest companie,
When after the *God-sauing* ceremonie,
For want of talke-stuffe, falls to foinerie,
Out goes his Rapier, and to *Liuia*,
He showes the ward by *puncta reuersa*.

The

Humours.

The *incarnata*. Nay, by the blessed light,
Before he goes, he'le teach her how to fight
And hold her weapon. Oh I laught amaine,
To see the madnes of this *Martius* vaine.
    But roome for *Tuscus*, that iest-mounging youth,
Who nere did ope his Apish gerning mouth
But to retaile and broke anothers wit.
Discourse of what you will, he straight can fit
Your present talke, with, *Sir, I'le tell a iest*,
(Of some sweet Lady, or graund Lord at least)
Then on he goes. And nere his tongue shall lie
Till his ingrossed iests are all drawne dry;
But then as dumbe as *Maurus*, when at play
H'ath lost his crownes, & paun'd his trim aray.
He doth naught but retaile iests, breake but one,
Out flies his table-booke, let him alone,
He'le haue't i-fayth; Lad, hast an Epigram,
Wilt haue it put into the chaps of Fame?

Giue

Humours.

Giue *Tuscus* coppies, sooth as his owne wit
His propper issue he will father it.
O that this Eccho, that doth speake, spet, write
Naught but the excrements of others spright,
This ill-stuft trunck of iests, whose very soule
Is but a heape of Iibes, should once inroule
His name mong creatures termed rationall,
vvhose chiefe repute, whose sence, whose soule & all
Are fed with offall scraps, that somtimes fall
From liberall wits, in their large festiuall.
  Come aloft Iack, roome for a vaulting skip.
Roome for *Torquatus*, that nere op'd his lip
But in prate of *pummado reuersa*,
Of the nimbling tumbling *Angelica*.
Now on my soule, his very intelect
Is naught but a curuetting *Sommerset*.
  Hush, hush, cryes (honest *Phylo*) peace, desist,
Doost thou not tremble sower Satyrist

Now

Humours.

Now iudiciall Musus *readeth thee?*
He'le whip each line, he'le scourge thy balladry,
Good fayth he will. Phylo I prethee stay
Whilst I the humour of this dogge display:
He's naught but censure, wilt thou credite me,
He neuer wrote one line in poesie,
But once at Athens in a theame did frame
A paradox in prayse of Vertues name,
Which still he hugs, and luls as tenderly
As cuckold *Tisus* his wifes bastardy.
Well, here's a challenge, I flatly say he lyes
That heard him ought but censure Poesies.
Tis his discourse, first hauing knit the brow,
Stroke vp his fore-top, champed euery row,
Belcheth his slauering censure on each booke
That dare presume euen on *Medusa* looke.
I haue no Artists skill in simphonies,
Yet when some pleasing Diapason flies

From

Humours.

From out the belly of a sweet touch'd Lute,
My eares dares say tis good, or when they sute
Some harsher seauens for varietie,
My natiue skill discernes it presently.
What then? will any sottish dolt repute
Or euer thinke me *Orpheus* absolute?
Shall all the world of Fidlers follow me,
Relying on my voyce in musickrie?
    Musus here's *Rhodes*, lets see thy boasted leape,
Or els avaunt lewd curre, presume not speake,
Or with thy venome-sputtering chaps to barke
Gainst well-pend Poems, in the tongue-tied darke.
    O for a humour, looke who yon doth goe,
The meager lecher, lewd *Luxurio*,
Tis he that hath the sole monopolie
By patent, of the Suburbe lecherie.
No new edition of drabbs comes out,
But seene and allow'd by *Luxurios* snout.

Did

Humours.

Did euer any man ere heare him talke
But of Pick-hatch, or of some Shorditch baulke,
Aretines filth, or of his wandring whore,
Of some *Cynedian*, or of *Tacedore*,
Of *Ruscus* nasty lothsome brothell rime,
That stinks like *Aiax* froth, or muck-pit slime.
The newes he tels you, is of some new flesh,
Lately broke vp, span new, hote piping fresh;
The curtesie he showes you, is some morne
To giue you *Venus* fore her smock be on.
His eyes, his tongue, his soule, his all is lust,
Which vengeance and confusion follow must.
Out on this salt humour, letchers dropsie,
Fie, it doth soile my chaster poesie.
  O spruce! How now *Piso*, *Aurelius* Ape,
What strange disguise, what new deformed shape
Doth hold thy thoughts in contemplation?
Faith say, what fashion art thou thinking on?

A

Humours.

A stitch'd Taffata cloake, a payre of slops
Of Spanish leather? O who heard his chops
Ere chew of ought, but of some strange disguise,
This fashion-mounger, each morne fore he rise
Contemplates sute shapes, & once frõ out his bed,
He hath them straight full liuely portrayed.
And then he chukes, and is as proud of this,
As *Taphus* when he got his neighbours blisse.
All fashions since the first yeere of this Queene,
May in his studdy fairely drawne be seene,
And all that shall be to his day of doome,
You may peruse within that little roome.
For not a fashion once dare show his face,
But from neate *Pyso* first must take his grace.
The long fooles coat,the huge slop,the lugg'd boot
From mimick *Pyso*, all doe claime their roote.
O that the boundlesse power of the soule
Should be coop'd vp in fashioning some roule!

But

Humours.

But ô, *Suffenus*, (that dooth hugge, imbrace
His propper selfe, admires his owne sweet face,
Prayseth his owne faire limmes proportion,
Kisseth his shade, recounteth all alone
His owne good parts) who enuies him? not I,
For well he may, without all riualrie.
  Fie, whether's fled my sprights alacritie?
How dull I vent this humorous poesie.
In faith I am sad, I am possest with ruth,
To see the vainenes of faire *Albions* youth;
To see their richest time euen wholy spent
In that which is but Gentries ornament.
Which being meanly done, becomes them well,
But when with deere times losse they doe excell,
How ill they doe things well. To daunce & sing,
To vault, to fence, & fairely trot a ring
With good grace, meanely done. O what repute
They doe beget, but being absolute,

It

Humours.

It argues too much time, too much regard
Imploy'd in that which might be better spard,
Then substance should be lost. If one should sew
For *Lesbias* loue, hauing two dayes to woe
And not one more, & should imploy those twaine
The fauour of her wayting-wench to gaine,
Were he not mad? Your apprehension,
Your wits are quicke in application.

     Gallants,
Me thinks your soules should grudge, & inly scorne
To be made slaue, to humors that are borne
In slime of filthy sensuality.
That part not subiect to mortality
(Boundlesse discursiue apprehension
Giuing it wings to act his function)
Me thinks shold murmur, whẽ you stop his course,
And soile his beauties in some beastly source,
         Of

Humours.

Of brutish pleasures. But it is so poore,
So weake, so hunger bitten, euermore
Kept from his foode, meagar for want of meate,
Scorn'd and reiected, thrust from out his seate,
Vpbray'd by Capons greace, consumed quite
By eating stewes, that waste the better spright.
Snib'd by his baser parts, that now poore *Soule*,
(Thus pesanted to each lewd thoughts controule)
Hath lost all hart, bearing all iniuries,
The vtmost spight, and rank'st indignities
With forced willingnes. Taking great ioy
If you will daine his faculties imploy
But in the mean'st ingenious quality.
(How proud he'le be of any dignity?)
Put it to musick, dauncing, fencing schoole,
Lord how I laugh to heare the pretty foole
How it will prate, his tongue shall neuer lie,
But still discourse of his spruce qualitie;

I.

Egging

Humours.

Egging his maister to proceed from this,
And get the substance of celestiall blisse.
His Lord straight calls his parliament of sence,
But still the sensuall haue preheminence.
The poore soules better part so feeble is,
So cold and dead is his *Synderesis*,
That shadowes by odde chaunce somtimes are got,
But ô the substance is respected not.
    Here ends my rage, though angry brow was bent
    Yet I haue sung in sporting merriment.

FINIS.

To euerlasting *Obli-uion*.

THou mighty gulfe, insatiat cormorant,
Deride me not, though I seeme petulant
To fall into thy chops. Let others pray
For euer their faire Poems flourish may.
But as for mee, hungry *Obliuion*
Deuoure me quick, accept my orizon:
My earnest prayers, which doe importune thee,
With gloomy shade of thy still Emperie,
To vaile both me and my rude poesie,

To euerlasting Obliuion.

Farre worthier lines in silence of thy state
Doe sleepe securely free from loue or hate,
From which this liuing, nere can be exempt,
But whilst it breathes will hate and fury tempt.
Then close his eyes with thy all-dimming hand,
Which not right glorious actions can with-stand.
Peace hatefull tongues, I now in silence pace,
Vnlesse some hound doe wake me from my place,
   I with this sharpe, yet well meant poesie,
   Will sleepe secure, right free from iniurie
   Of cancred hate, or rankest villanie.

To

To him that hath peru-
sed mee.

Entle, or vngentle hand that holdest mee, let not thine eye be cast vpon priuatnes, for I protest I glaunce not on it. If thou hast perused mee, what lesser fauour canst thou graunt then not to abuse me with vniust application? Yet I feare mee, I shall be much, much, iniuried by two sorts of readers: the one being ignorant, not knowing the nature of a Satyre, (which is vnder fained priuate names, to note generall vices,) vvill needes wrest each fayned name to a priuate vnfained person. The other too subtile, bearing a priuate malice to some greater personage then hee dare in his ovvne person seeme to malingne, will striue by a forced application of my generall reproofes to broach his priuate hatred. Then the

I 3   which

To the Peruser

which I know not a greater iniury can be offered to a
Satyrist. I durst presume, knew they how guiltlesse,
and how free I were from prying into priuatnes, they
would blush to thinke, hovv much they wrong them
selues in seeking to iniure mee. Let this protestation
satisfie our curious searchers. So may I obtayne my
best hopes, as I am free from endeuouring to blast any
priuate mans good name. If any one (forced with his
owne guilt) will turne it home and say *Tis I,* I cannot
hinder him. Neyther doe I iniure him. For other
faults of Poesie, I craue no pardon, in that I scorne all
pennance the bitterest censurer can impose vpon mee.
Thus (wishing each man to leaue enquiring who I am,
and learne to know himselfe,) I take a solemne congee
of this fusty world.

Theriomastix.

ERRATA

The following emendations have been made in the text of the original:—

Page	Line		In the Original reads :
3	1	' *indignos* '	' *indgnos* '
20	18	' *change)* '	' *change !* '
26	12	' *heauen* '	' *heaueu* '
35⎫ 36⎭	1	' *risisti* '	' *ricisti* '
40	6	' *Aquinians* '	' *Aquimians* '
43	3	' sympathie. '	' sympathie, '
44	13	' oppugn'st '	' oppung'st '
49	11	' words '	' word '
93	9	' Oration,) '	' Oration,'
98	12	' intermell '	' ietermell '
113	11	' her '	' his '
117	6	' Vpbrayd '	' Npbrayd.'

NOTE

AS I have suggested that Jaques in *As You Like It* may owe something to Marston, it may not be out of place to consider the possibility more fully. There is, indeed, occasionally an air of mystery about Jaques. For the most part he remains his own incomparable, melancholy self; but once or twice in *As You Like It*, Shakespeare appears to forget that he is Jaques and indulges in what seems to be comment on passing affairs. This is especially noticeable in Act II, Sc. 7, when Jaques defends himself against the Duke's accusation:

> 'Why, who cries out on pride,
>   That can therein tax any private party?
>   Doth it not flow as hugely as the sea
>   Till that the wearer's very means do ebb?
>   What woman in the city do I name,
>   When that I say the city woman bears
>   The cost of princes on unworthy shoulders?
>   Who can come in and say that I mean her,
>   When such a one as she such is her neighbour?
>   Or what is he of basest function,
>   That says his bravery is not on my cost,
>   Thinking that I mean him, but therein suits
>   His folly to the mettle of my speech?
>   There then; how then? what then? Let me see
>   wherein
>   My tongue hath wronged him: if it do him right,
>   Then he hath wronged himself; if he be free,
>   Why then my taxing like a wild-goose flies
>   Unclaim'd of any man.'

This speech looks very like a piece of literary politics,

especially when it is placed alongside the closing paragraph, 'To him that hath perused me,' in *The Scourge of Villanie.*

Now most editors place the first performance of *As You Like It* in this same year 1599, and one of the reasons they give for the date is Celia's remark, that since 'the little wit that fools have is silenced, the little fooling that wise men have makes a great show'—which is plausibly taken to refer to the burning of the satirical books. It is, therefore, not improbable that Shakespeare is gently satirising his melancholy contemporary in the person of Jaques.

Such identifications, however, are rather a dangerous snare, and often lead editors to make too exact parallels. Personal allusions are common enough in Elizabethan drama, but dramatists do not often introduce characters which *consistently* caricature living individuals. For the most part there is a name, a parody, an odd gag, or an unmistakable gesture, and then the character steps back again into his proper place in the plot.

However, whether Shakespeare does or does not touch Marston in this scene, the origin of the name of Jaques is fairly clear. It comes by an underground, not to say cloacal, channel from Sir John Harrington's *Metamorphosis of Ajax* (1596). Harrington was writing a scientific treatise on domestic sanitation in a Rabelaisian strain, and he used the name Ajax for the household offices. Thus, as he explains, AIAX = A IAX = A IAKES. But there is another connection between Ajax and a jakes; both are melancholy, like the 'melancholy of Moorditch' and such unsavoury similes.

Now Ajax is the classic type of the Melancholick Humour. Harrington says in his Prologue that Ajax, after his unsuccessful attack on Ulysses, 'coulde indure it no longer but became a perfect mal-content, viz. his hat without a band, his hose without garters, his wast without a girdle, his bootes without spurs, his purse without coyne, his heade without wit, and thus swearing he would kill & slay: First he kild all horned beasts . . .' etc.

The connection between Jaques, Ajax, and jakes can be brought still closer, for Harrington tells another story.

'There was a very tall and seruiciable Gentleman, sometime Lieutenant of the ordinance, called M. *Iaques Wingfield*; who comming one day, either of businesse, or of kindnes, to visit a great Lady in the Court, the Lady bad her gentlewoman aske, which of the *Wingfields* it was, hee tolde her *Iaques Wingfield*: the modest gentlewoman, that was not so well seene in the Frenche, to knowe that *Iaques* was but *Iames* in English, who so bashfoole, that to mend the matter (as she thought) she brought her Lady worde, not without blushing, that it was M. *Priuie Wingfield*, of which, I suppose the Lady then, I am sure the Gentleman after, as long as hee liued, was wont to make great sport.' (Sig. B7.)

'Jaques,' then, is not an inappropriate name for the melancholy philosopher to whom the Duke said:

'For thou thyself hast been a libertine,
    As sensual as the brutish sting itself;
    And all th' embossed sores and headed evils,
    That thou with license of free foot hast caught,
    Wouldst thou disgorge into the general world.'

But 'Old Jakes' is a still better name for the author of *The Scourge of Villanie.*

GAYLORD M-2   PRINTED IN U.S.A.